The Invincible Soul

The Invincible Soul

Pt. Girdhari Lal Salwan—A Biography

Mohinder Singh ◆ Indu Khetarpal

HARPER
VANTAGE

First published in India in 2012 by Harper Vantage
An imprint of HarperCollins *Publishers* India
a joint venture with
The India Today Group

Copyright © Salwan Education Trust 2012

ISBN: 978-93-5029-583-0

2 4 6 8 10 9 7 5 3 1

HarperCollins *Publishers*
A-53, Sector 57, Noida, Uttar Pradesh 201301, India
77-85 Fulham Palace Road, London W6 8JB, United Kingdom
Hazelton Lanes, 55 Avenue Road, Suite 2900, Toronto, Ontario M5R 3L2
and 1995 Markham Road, Scarborough, Ontario M1B 5M8, Canada
25 Ryde Road, Pymble, Sydney, NSW 2073, Australia
31 View Road, Glenfield, Auckland 10, New Zealand
10 East 53rd Street, New York NY 10022, USA

Typeset in 12/16 PalmSprings Regular at
SÜRYA

Printed and bound at
Thomson Press (India) Ltd.

Dedicated to each and every member of the Salwan Schools, the members of the community who have knowingly or unknowingly worked to further the legacy of the founder, and the Salwan Education Trust, driven by the mission, 'Education for All'

Contents

Foreword

The Partition and its horrors continue to live on in memory. It is the reason, on the one hand, for the nostalgia that has led the people of India and Pakistan to light candles on the border to ignite friendship and, on the other, for the enmity that has provoked four wars between the two countries.

It was the biggest migration in the world with no Moses to lead the people. The tale of every migrant is a saga of sacrifice and suffering and also a story of betrayal, friendship and community. I do not know what the verdict of posterity will be, but none can blind themselves to the harrowing experience the migrants went through. The government on both sides was settling down to post-Partition realities. People felt cheated. They were shattered, beleaguered and disillusioned. They were refugees, yet determined to go ahead.

Luckily, those who came from the North West Frontier Province (NWFP), the land of the Frontier Gandhi, Khan Abdul Ghaffar Khan, found in Girdhari Lal Salwan a selfless leader. He helped them stand tall once again. Rehabilitation Minister Mehr Chand Khanna, also from the NWFP, knew how honest and transparent Girdhari Lal was. He entrusted him with the task of distributing financial assistance to the people from that region. The sum was paltry, but Girdhari Lal's words of encouragement were in abundance.

Indeed, Girdhari Lal performed miracles that are recorded in history. He persuaded the government to build the Rajendra Nagar colony in Delhi. What was initially a row of tents became a throbbing place with 'pucca' houses and busy markets. Those who were once penniless refugees are now millionaires.

But Girdhari Lal's real passion was education. He was known for establishing schools and imparting a high standard of education. The Salwan Education Trust, registered in early 1950 in Delhi, was his contribution to free India. He re-established the Salwan School on the same lines as the institution he had founded in 1943 in Peshawar. Today, there are as many as eleven Salwan Schools, catering to 10,000 students, offering them the best of teachers and the finest facilities.

The Invincible Soul gives some glimpses of his dedicated and relentless work to help the helpless. The book is a tribute to his efforts. But books cannot encompass and throw complete light on the magnitude of what he handled and accomplished. His memory is embedded deep in the minds of people and his name has and will be taken with reverence for generations to come.

December 2012   KULDIP NAYAR
New Delhi

Preface

Lives of great men all remind us we can make our lives sublime.
And, departing, leave behind us footprints on the sands of time.

—Henry Wadsworth Longfellow

Ever since mankind created language, it has been the unabated endeavour of the human race to record history and celebrate personalities – great people who have left their mark on the sands of time. Many came and contributed to their present, many changed the way we look at the past, and many left behind a vision for the future. A select few created a continuum between the past, present and future with exemplary work that is even today being carried forward, driven by the same mission that was charted decades ago. An exceptional name in this regard is that of Pandit Girdhari Lal Salwan. He stands tall in the list of pioneers who contributed to the setting up of educational institutions and left behind a legacy that guides and illuminates the way for one and all. Every brick of the Salwan Schools in Delhi, Gurgaon and Ghaziabad whispers his ideology, ensuring that it is mingled with the ethos of the school.

Pandit Girdhari Lal Salwan was the perfect embodiment of the five elements of earth, water, fire, air and space, which gave him a sense of interconnectedness, impermanence, and insubstantiality, as if acknowledging how life is an ever-changing process rather than a static thing to which one can cling. Recognizing this, the equanimity of his existence is best demonstrated by looking at the journey of his life superimposed on these elements.

The Invincible Soul is an effort to pay tribute to a man who stood for equality in education, and who did so with unparalleled passion, grit and determination. This biography is an attempt to give readers a glimpse into the life and times of an educationist who dared to put aside his personal tragedies, pitfalls and political ups and downs for his commitment to the cause, 'Education for All.'

The source material for this biography has been provided by Shiv Dutt Salwan and verified by the present Trustees. We prepared this volume in deference to the wishes of Shiv Dutt Salwan as a labour of love and we do hope this will inspire the youth in different parts of India and abroad.

We would like to express our gratitude to Shiv Dutt Salwan for having spared his valuable time to record the incidents relating to the life and times of the founder of Salwan Schools. We are also thankful to the Salwan Educational Trust for its continued support in the preparation of this volume and to Kuldip Nayar for writing the foreword.

December 2012   MOHINDER SINGH
New Delhi   INDU KHETARPAL

A Humble Beginning

An Invocation

*Life of my Life, I shall ever try
to keep my body pure, knowing that thy living touch
is upon all my limbs.*

*I shall ever try to keep all untruths out of my thoughts,
knowing that thou art that truth which has kindled
the light of reason in my mind.*

*I shall ever try to drive all evils away from my heart
and keep my love in flower, knowing that thou hast thy seat
in the inmost shrine of my heart.*

*And it shall be my endeavour to reveal thee in my actions,
knowing it is thy power that gives me strength to act.*

—Rabindranath Tagore
Gitanjali/Lyric 4

A young Girdhari Lal faces down the angry mahant of Gurdwara Tham Sahib, Kartarpur, 1918.

Once Upon a Time in Kartarpur

Kartarpur, 1918: Every evening, the market came alive with large crowds of people unwinding after a tiring day. Families would look forward to this time of day, even going so far as to dress up for the evening session of gossip and chatter.

But every day, as if on cue, this lively chatter was disrupted. The buggy of the mahant would storm into the market like a mad elephant, making everyone, young and old, run for cover. Not one of them dared oppose the mahant of Gurdwara Tham Sahib.

Things continued this way until one day, a sixteen-year-old boy decided it was time for change.

It was a warm July evening and the carriage came with its usual arrogance, oblivious to the people around. Suddenly, the boy darted forward and stopped the carriage by gripping the reins of the horse. Furious, the coachman whipped the horse as a warning to the boy, but he refused to budge. The mahant shouted, 'Do you want to commit suicide?' Without flinching, the boy said, 'If you promise to ride slowly I will leave the reins!'

Enraged by his defiance, the mahant ordered the coachman to whip the boy into obedience. Lashing out in a mad frenzy, the coachman whipped the boy, but he refused to yield his ground. Finally, realizing that force would prove futile, the mahant asked the coachman to relent and promised that the carriage would be driven with care in the future. As he left, he looked the boy over with admiration and asked 'What is your name?'. 'Girdhari Lal Salwan, son of Pandit Mool Raj Salwan,' he replied.

This incident displayed Girdhari Lal's courage and

Pandit Mool Raj Salwan, father of Girdhari Lal.

selflessness, qualities that would shine all the more brightly as he grew up.

The Birth of a Karmayogi

Kartarpur, meaning the 'City of God,' is a town near Jalandhar. It is located in the Doaba region of Punjab. It was founded by the fifth guru of the Sikhs, Guru Arjan Dev.

With the passage of time, the guru's abode became a place dedicated to service of the needy. It was a natural choice of residence for Mool Raj Salwan and his wife after the former's retirement from the Indian Railways. Mool Raj considered it a blessing to live in a place that was known as the abode of God. For him, Kartapur's rich past promised an equally rich and fulfilling future.

Grandson of a well respected commander in the army of Maharaja Ranjit Singh, Mool Raj soon earned a reputation for honesty, discipline and as an upholder of family values. The persona of Mool Raj was complemented by his calm and compassionate wife, Hukam Devi. The neighbourhood soon became home for Mool Raj Salwan, Hukam Devi and their seven children.

The sixth child was born on 5 December 1902. His arrival was celebrated by the entire neighbourhood. The proud parents named him Girdhari, another name for Lord Krishna. Little did the family or the community realize that they were celebrating the birth of a great son who would grow up to be a crusader dedicated to the betterment of society.

The young Girdhari never had any craving for material wealth. He was motivated by the most intangible assets that he inherited and imbibed from his parents, and learned early the value of a good education. Both Mool Raj and Hukam Devi took great care to make their children understand the importance of self-esteem. Nurtured in such a supportive and cultured environment, the children grew up to be confident human beings with a keen sense of moral discernment and strong character.

But like the cycle of day and night, life is filled with its cups of happiness and sorrow, and the Salwan family was no exception to this law. Tragedy struck when the couple lost four of their sons to disease. Misfortune continued when their only daughter, Parvati, was widowed within three years of her marriage. Shortly after that, the couple lost their fifth son as well. Girdhari remained the sole surviving son. The experience tempered his body and mind to face the world with renewed vigour.

Pragmatic and open to confronting prevailing social attitudes, Mool Raj and Hukam Devi decided to get Parvati married for the second time. They were branded as outcastes and threatened with ostracism. In spite of this, the couple stood firm. It was Parvati who refused to marry again. Instead, she sought solace in the teachings of her parents and mustered the courage to live out her days as a single woman. She took to social work, supporting the emancipation of women from prejudiced customs and inhibitions.

Mool Raj and Hukam Devi chose to draw strength from their adversities rather than admit defeat and wallow in bitterness. With retirement from active service in the offing, Mool Raj began to invest his time in woodwork. Little did he realize that this hobby would become the foundation for an enduring business. Such a vocation was considered a menial task for Brahmins and, as expected, made the Salwans vulnerable to criticism. Mool Raj, being faithful to his newly found passion, changed the paradigm and seized the opportunity to educate the Brahmins about the curative powers of wood carvings and the therapeutic potential of physical labour.

His determination and single-mindedness soon silenced his detractors. Manual labour served to strengthen his bond with nature. Being an absolute novice, the amateur status drove him to work hard and become a professional. His entry into the carving business became the harbinger of change, providing the family with a sustainable vocation. Within a short span of time, Mool Raj Salwan created a niche for himself in the wood carving and furniture market. He set a precedent for everyone and proved to the community that a Brahmin, irrespective of his inherited status, can handle other professions as successfully as those traditionally associated with his caste. As a result, Kartarpur is famous for furniture even today.

Creating a Business in Peshawar

Mool Raj Salwan had a canny eye for the business potential of the furniture industry; he was well aware of the needs of the Indian nobility and elite, as well as the British hankering for anything that suggested the rich heritage of India's culture. This knack for reading the market fuelled his production, and soon he became a celebrated name for creating masterpieces from wood. Further, he perfected the art to the level of customization wherein he reoriented the designs as per the taste and preference of his customers. Mool Raj slowly attained the status of a leader and artisan who was a master of his trade.

Pandit Girdhari Lal Salwan in his younger days.

Meanwhile, Girdhari Lal was growing up, and learning to balance his focus and time between the furniture business and family responsibilities. Having been compelled to discontinue studies due to the family circumstances, he had taken on the responsibility of supporting the families of his brothers. The fruits of his labour gradually paid off as Girdhari Lal successfully made his own place in the hearts of his father's ever-growing list of clients.

Girdhari Lal worked within a business framework that was not driven by profit. He examined the work orders coming his way in the larger context of a value-oriented system. This was the major difference between his manner of looking at business, and that of a more conventional, profit-minded entrepreneur. He quickly picked up the skills of the wood shaping trade. The business started yielding good results, motivating him to put in even more hours and enhanced effort.

Mool Raj was proud of his son's keen interest and capabilities in the business. As a father, he wanted Girdhari to have a larger canvas, a larger playing field, and advised him to shift his business from Kartarpur to Peshawar in the North West Frontier Province (NWFP), then a flourishing cantonment town. This shift, undertaken in 1921, marked a turning point in the family's fortune.

Girdhari Lal's independent journey began when his father died soon after his move to Peshawar. He matured into a person who felt driven to fulfil his responsibilities towards his family, a person who wanted to live a fuller life, with a major share of his time dedicated to serving the cause of others. He turned the greater part of his attention from business ventures to those aimed at promoting and protecting societal welfare.

As his furniture business prospered, he spent more and more of his income on social welfare projects. Girdhari Lal successfully turned his ordinary background into an extraordinary and inspirational story. He developed a reputation for the quality and workmanship of his furniture.

Girdhari Lal's furniture business rose to new heights as he achieved a fine balance between competence, professionalism and ethical practices in the trade. He built a furniture showroom (above) in Peshawar in 1944.

If any piece of furniture was not up to the mark set by his evaluation standards, it would not be put up for sale. He strove to achieve the highest possible benchmark in manufacturing quality, giving due importance to the concept of an involved, well motivated worker and client. If a piece did not meet the most exacting quality standards, he would de-list the piece by defacing it on the shop floor itself. His son Shiv Dutt still keeps in touch with some of the old customers who had bought furniture from his father's showroom in Peshawar, sixty or seventy years earlier. These old customers consider the pieces of furniture their cherished possessions even today and approach the Salwans for getting the same re-polished or repaired.

Girdhari Lal's furniture was in great demand even amongst the British social elite and officers. Before they left India (when they were transferred or commissioned back to England), some of them ordered furniture from the Salwans for their homes in England. Girdhari Lal would customize special folding furniture for them. Almost all the furniture in the governor's house in NWFP was supplied by him. Girdhari Lal had established his credibility as a fine craftsman; he built a furniture showroom and a workshop. This was in the cantonment area of Peshawar and was completed during the period 1944-45.

A Man of Discipline

Girdhari Lal was a man of simple habits with a well regulated routine. He would get up at four in the morning, and jog four miles with his wife and children to the 'Gorakhnath Chashma', where the water was cool in summer and warm in winter. He attached great importance to physical fitness, which was reflected in his dietary habits and meticulous exercise routine. As part of the regime he did five hundred squats every day. The children enjoyed this early morning outing and swim. Girdhari Lal wanted his children to exercise regularly, for he believed in the principle of 'a sound mind in a sound body'. 'If young children go out on such physical exercises in the morning,' he used to say, 'they will keep away from evil and have better concentration and focus in life.'

His eating habits were equally well regulated. After a cup of tea and two pieces of toast, he had a frugal lunch of two chapattis, which would come to his workplace from home, and a glass of milk for dinner. He never ate anything from outside and managed with some biscuits and tea when he went out. He was a pure vegetarian as well as a teetotaller, and he never smoked. According to his daughter, Ved Rani, he never fell ill or had common ailments like coughs, colds or stomach aches. He was advised by a hakeem of Kartarpur to eat less in order to live longer and healthier. After that, he refrained from taking dinner. He was often heard advising his friends, 'The human body does not need the quantity of food people normally eat. Eating more than what the body needs is a bad habit and those who eat too much get sick. People do not die because they are hungry, but because of excessive eating.'

He was aware of the danger of burnout and adhered to his system of mental stress relief through prayers, relaxation and being close to nature. He arranged his daily schedule so as to spend some time with his children, family and friends. Girdhari Lal and his wife, Gyan Devi, were blessed with five children—

three sons and two daughters. His son, Brahm Dutt, was the eldest, followed by Santosh Rani, Shiv Dutt, Ved Rani and the youngest, Ramesh Dutt.

At this point, Girdhari Lal led a blissful life—he had been nurtured by loving parents, he had overcome the challenges that motivate a person to give his best, he had developed a business model which had the promise of a great future and he had a loving and affectionate family. Little did he realize that he was embarking upon a lifelong journey that would present him with an opportunity to further the cause of education for his children and find his own mission in life.

The Evolving Self

An Invocation

*When the heart is hard and parched, come upon me
with a shower of mercy.*

When grace is lost from life, come with a burst of song.

*When tumultuous work raises its din on all sides
shutting me out from beyond, come to me, my lord of
silence, with thy peace and rest.*

*When my beggarly heart sits crouched, shut up
in a corner, break open the door, my king, and come
with the ceremony of a king.*

*When desire blinds the mind with delusion and dust,
O thou holy one, thou wakeful, come with thy light
and thy thunder.*

—Rabindranath Tagore
Gitanjali/Lyric 39

The Birth of an Educationist

Girdhari Lal was undergoing a process of rapid transformation and facing multiple demands on his time. These were business interests, social alleviation programmes and his doting love and care for the family. Prime amongst all the considerations was his concern for the future and education of his children. While the children were growing up, Girdhari Lal was trying to understand, in his own right, the responsibilities that come with parenthood. Prime amongst these was the concern to provide his children a stable foundation with the best of education. This was difficult for him since he had not been able to educate himself, though that had been due to circumstances beyond his control. Though bereft of the benefits of a formal education, Girdhari Lal was well aware of the importance of his own efforts towards providing his children what he himself had lacked. Education for him became an immediate task in the context of his children and a life mission undertaken for the benefit of society.

Education in those days was considered more of a status symbol than an imperative for good upbringing. Thus, it was viewed as a privilege and a fashionable necessity for the rich and the elite. The Peshawar cantonment of the pre-Independence years had only two major schools. Girdhari Lal tried very hard to get two of his sons admitted to the Convent of Jesus and Mary (boys were admitted only up to the fifth standard in the convent). His sons were denied admission simply because he was neither an officer nor had titles like 'Rai Sahib' or 'Rai Bahadur.' He repeatedly met the principal but was politely shown the door each time on the pretext of steep tuition fees or was stalled and told to come and try his luck another month.

Then came a day when the frivolous excuses stopped. Girdhari Lal got his first taste of 'apartheid' when he was told bluntly by the principal, 'Hum ek carpenter ke bacchon ko admission de ke acche ghar ke bacchon ka bhavishya kharab nahi kar sakte' (We cannot admit children of a carpenter and spoil the future of the children from good families). Confronted with a bias based merely upon a social divide, Girdhari Lal knew that he had reached a dead end as far as good schools were concerned. Nevertheless, he refused to let the prejudice of the schools dampen his hope in his children's future. He knew that his prayers would be answered. The resolve was so strong in his mind that the seeds of a dream school were sown, waiting for an opportunity to flower.

Giving Education a Chance

Peshawar of those days bore testimony to a lot of monopolistic practices which had their genesis in the economic divides that riddled the society. The fortification of such practices was pivotal to the further widening of these gaps. Girdhari Lal found himself battling these preconceptions and entrenched prejudices as he searched for avenues to further the educational interest of his children. Little did he realize that he was on the threshold of creating an opportunity not only for his children but for a larger segment of society.

At that time, the two schools Convent of Jesus and Mary and St. John's in Peshawar were, in a manner of speaking, reserved for the children of the elite. Added to this was the fact that the boarding schools in Lahore and Rawalpindi were patronized only by the rich class on account of extremely high fees. Consequently, the major share of imparting education fell on the shoulders of Frontier, Islamia and Sanatan Dharam schools. Before 1938, there was only one high school in the Peshawar cantonment where the Hindus and the Muslims studied together. Many a time there were quarrels of a communal nature. The atmosphere was totally Islamic. Nothing was taught about the Hindu religion and heroes. The Sanatan Dharam Sabha started a boys high school and a girls high school to cater to religious and educational needs of the Hindus and the Sikhs. These schools were jointly managed by both communities. Later, the Sikhs started their own Khalsa School.

Girdhari Lal had a strong standing with the association which managed the Sanatan Dharam mandir. He was also in the management committee of Sanatan Dharam School. At the time, the school was struggling to survive: it was faced with an acute financial crunch and inadequate infrastructure, with just eight classrooms being operated from a hired building. The building itself was in a dilapidated state and far below the mark. The decaying façade was only the first sign of various other deficiencies. The school was finding it extremely difficult to fulfil the recognition requirements charted out in the erstwhile 'Punjab Education Code'. According to the requirements, the school needed to have trained teachers with regular salaries, a proper building and a playground.

The temple and the committee were running out of options and ideas to honour the requirements. With no system of government grants in place, the odds were heavily stacked against the survival of the school. The situation became grim with the disproportionate equation of the low fee structure and the relatively higher salary scales of the teachers as laid out in the education code. This was creating a huge gap between the fees of students forming the inflow and the rightful salary of the teachers as per the standard scales. So when the school housed grades up till class VIII, it did not come as a surprise that the education officer refused to recognize it. The management finally had to bow down to the decision to close the school.

In view of the impending closure, the government issued a circular advising parents to shift their children to other schools. Alternately, the government offered to allot land for the school, provided the managing committee agreed to the provision for a proper building and playground. Keeping this condition in sight, the general body made one last attempt at their meeting to preserve the school. The meeting was attended by prominent leaders of the Hindu community, such as rich Rai Bahadurs and other British title-holders, but when it came to building the school everyone looked the other way. No one wanted to part with his money, knowing fully well that their own wards would go to other schools, so why invest in this school? The writing on the wall was clear. Given this, they were almost unanimous in the decision that the community should give up the idea of running their own school, certainly if it involved investments.

The meeting of the general body turned out to be a well rehearsed performance being led to a foregone conclusion, when someone asked an unexpected question, 'But is there anyone who could build a school?' While everyone was quiet, the silence was pierced by the authoritative voice of Girdhari Lal: 'Yes, I will build the school.' There was a hush in the hall.

'Kya! Ek carpenter school building banayega?' (Will a carpenter build the school building?) many of them asked mockingly. With heavy sarcasm, Rai Bahadur Dina Nath said, 'If you think you can build a school in six months, we will allow you to do so.' The hush in the hall was followed by questioning looks from the committee members. Girdhari Lal stood up to the challenge, nodding his head, eyes gleaming with thrill. His confident gait silenced those who had uttered cynical and sarcastic words. He stepped out in the scorching sun and drew energy from the heavens as if charging himself for the battle ahead.

Embracing the Life Mission

The school project became a life mission for Girdhari Lal. He was conscious of the fact that he had to create an excellent building and playground with the right kind of environment, wherein holistic education could be nurtured. He was aware of the stipulations of the education code and was determined to ensure total compliance with the provisions to build a model institute. He could envision the larger role of the educationist beyond the bare infrastructural provisions and he set about the task in a focused manner. He was conscious of the role of education in the larger societal objective. He was also aware that there would be no place for mediocrity in the project.

With a strong and determined mind, he set out to fulfil his task. From resourcing building materials to coordinating with contractors, architects, planners; from hiring teachers to designing uniforms, Girdhari Lal did not leave any stone unturned. He was a man seized by ambition to make the school a role model for its peers. So unique was his thinking that he saw the school uniform as a medium to break the barriers of class, creed and caste. Despite the fact that he was living in a rented house, Girdhari Lal invested all that he earned on the school building and completed the project.

By the time the school building was completed in 1943, Girdhari Lal had spent more than a few lakhs. At that period of time this was a huge sum. The school was appropriately named 'Salwan Sanatan Dharam High School'. The building was a great piece of architecture. The governor of NWFP, Sir George Cunningham, in his inaugural address said, 'I am pleased to see this school. I wish I had been lucky enough to study in such a beautiful school. I wish for many such schools in my province.' The governor also showered praise on the founder of Salwan Sanatan Dharam High School, saying 'I have never seen such an honest, sincere, and hardworking man of high character.' By this time, Girdhari Lal's concern for his fellow human beings, his conviction to take up challenges and his creativity had manifested itself in the erection of two beautiful school buildings. He would only progress and make more efforts to further that spirit in the years to come.

As an educationist, he believed that the purpose of education was to ensure growth of a student in all dimensions: mental, physical and spiritual. For the fulfilment of these objectives he carved out a multidisciplinary curriculum which ensured all-round development. The curriculum ensured that all students imbibed high moral values along with receiving an exposure to sports. He would lead the school teams to inter-school matches and ensure an active involvement of the managing committee to cheer the students and keep their motivation levels high. At the same time, he was particular about value education. His personal belief in self discipline became the doctrine for the school and everyone was taught the value of punctuality and respect for time.

Having accepted the challenge before the committee, Girdhari Lal honoured his commitment by creating an exemplary school. He won the hearts of people and was soon looked upon as an educationist with a magic wand. He gained tremendous confidence and credibility in the social sphere. Even the toughest of his critics acknowledged his achievement with genuine respect and sincere accolades. Having witnessed his success with one school, the general body decided to thrust another task upon him. Sanatan Dharam Girls School too was in a deep financial crisis and was facing closure. The temple committee requested Girdhari Lal to take over the management of the school and resolve its issues. Soon both the schools became the shining stars of the Peshawar cantonment. According to Shiv Dutt, 'the school buildings were a visual delight for one and all.'

The schools were not confined to the education of the minorities. Once, addressing his teachers, Girdhari Lal said, 'The greatest quality of a teacher is to be fair to all sections of society. The teacher should view every child equally, whether the child is rich or poor, Hindu or Muslim, high or low class. The child of a peon is in no way inferior to my own child. You should educate him in such a way that he should feel proud of himself and become self-confident. He should never feel inferior to the students of another school.'

The following prayer was recited every Friday during the morning assembly:

21

Lab pe aati hai dua ban ke tamanna meri (Urdu)

Lab pe aati hai dua ban ke tamanna meri
Zindagi shama ki surat ho khudaya meri
Door duniya ka mere dam se andhera ho jaye
Har jagah mere chamakne se ujala ho jaye
Ho mere dum se yun hi mere watan ki zeenat
Jis tarah phool se hoti hai chaman ki zeenat
Zindagi ho meri parwaane ki soorat ya rab
ilm ki shama se ho mujhko mohabbat ya rab
Ho mera kaam ghareebon ki himayat karna
Dardmandon se, zaeefon se muhabbat karna
Mere Allah! buraee se bachana mujhko
Naik jo raah ho us reh pe chalana mujhko.

—Janab Allama Iqbal

It translates into English thus:

With a prayer on my lips comes the yearning for an enlightened life,
May darkness be dispelled from the earth,
By my indomitable spirit to spread brightness,
Like a flower that accentuates the beauty of a garden,
Pray the beauty of my nation be adorned by my life-breath
Help me God, to focus on my life,
And be enraptured with knowledge,
Like the everlasting fascination of shama-parvana,
May the mission of my life be to help the poor,
Bestow love to those in pain and need
My Creator! Deliver me from all evil and
Help me to tread on the path of righteousness.

22

Girdhari Lal vowed to impart education to all, to the poor and needy, free of cost. Parents realized the merit of sending their children to a school where only 'value based education' would be imparted. Soon the student strength swelled to 800 plus. Amidst all the instabilities of the 1940s in India, the schools continued to surge ahead and became a prominent and important feature of Peshawar. The popularity of Girdhari Lal rose, and people started calling him 'Panditji'. He was invited to religious, social and political functions where he communicated with people of distinction. People also approached him for help, which he gave liberally without any hesitation or discrimination.

The First Committee of Salwan Education Trust (SET)

After the success of these models, Girdhari Lal realized that the schools should get focused attention, and be managed by dedicated management units. At the same time, he felt the need for having a body or a group of people who could think proactively towards the larger issues in education. He also envisioned that this team would play a strong role in forging a connection between education and society. At the same time, the policymakers were already thinking of an 'integrated' approach towards education. Hence, Girdhari Lal set up the Salwan Education Committee in 1938 (subsequently registered as Salwan Education Trust).

The management dedicated itself to the promotion of an 'integrated education' with a vision geared towards a better future. Their experience and expertise created a platform for sending forth pupils with sound character, essential for the nation's resurgence. At Peshawar, the schools were run

The first batch of students along with the staff of
Salwan Sanatan Dharam High School in Peshawar cantonment, 1943.

by a managing committee with Girdhari Lal as the president. The members of the committee were experts in diverse fields, and showed unflinching commitment to the cause of education.

- Mehr Chand Khanna — Patron
- Girdhari Lal Salwan — President
- Rai Sahib Badri Nath Talwar — Member
- Rai Bahadur Dina Nath — Member
- Rai Sahib Roora Ram — Member
- Vaishno Das Sethi — Member
- Suraj Prakash — Member
- Master Hari Ram — Member

With the formation of the Salwan Education Committee, Girdhari Lal was presented with the opportunity of widening his social network and attracting more and more expertise to the school while cutting across various social segments. This established Girdhari Lal among the most respected social figures. However, he remained as humble as he had always been. The then deputy commissioner of Peshawar, Sir Sikandar Mirza (who later had the honour of becoming the president of Pakistan), wished to decorate Girdhari Lal with the title of 'Rai Sahib'. He declined the offer. The British government realized that Girdhari Lal deserved bigger honours and therefore wanted to confer the title of 'Rai Bahadur' on him but this was also politely declined. Anyone else in his unique position would have been attracted to such titles and the social status that came with them, but not Girdhari Lal, who retained his humility even after being acknowledged as 'worthy' of so many distinctions.

Challenging Injustice

Every social movement has its followers and some of these followers rise above the rest to qualify as defining catalysts of the movement. Girdhari Lal was blessed to be one such significant agent of change as the rank and file of society looked upon him as their leader. His popularity as an educationist and his status as a socially conscious and capable individual made him a prominent citizen in more ways than one.

As a significant member of the general body of Sanatan Dharam School, his life changed completely. The Arya Samaj started the practice of satyagrah in the period 1938-39. Girdhari Lal's commitment to society had a great impact on his sons, making them socially aware and active at a tender age. Girdhari Lal allowed his sons Brahm Dutt, fifteen years, and Shiv Dutt, eleven years, to enrol in the first batch of satyagrahis from Peshawar to protest against the Nizam of Hyderabad's ban on *Satyartha Prakash* (a book written by

Swami Dayanand Saraswati, founder of the Arya Samaj) in 1875 .

It is believed that it was under the influence of the Razakars and other fundamentalists that the Nizam of Hyderabad had banned *Satyartha Prakash*. The genesis of the problem was that Swami Dayanand Saraswati, as part of his observations, had pointed out certain factors in all religions (including Hinduism) which he considered 'wrong beliefs and unscientific foundations'. The Muslim fundamentalists took exception to certain pronouncements and protested. As a consequence, the Nizam of Hyderabad imposed a ban on the book. This led to large-scale agitation, with satyagrahis from all over the country congregating at Hyderabad (now the capital of Andhra Pradesh). Going a step further, the Nizam had imprisoned 16,000 people and had also imposed restrictions on certain activities and rights of the Hindus. This was considered an attack on Hinduism.

Swami Dayanand had spoken about shuddhi or purification, implying that people who were converted to Islam by force should be brought back to the Hindu fold through this process. The atmosphere was very charged and tense, leading to extreme sensitivity. The non-converted Hindus were upset to discover that their very own brethren were arrayed against them. They wanted justice, freedom, and, above all, brotherhood.

People were pitched against each other in a communal frenzy with the masses looking for some intervention, some sense of refuge and rationalization. Girdhari Lal could see that the British policy of 'divide and rule' was at work. He knew that the only way out was to channelize this 'blind fury' into an organized protest. He believed that satyagraha was the only recourse which could give vent to the community's feelings without unleashing them in a violent frenzy. Leading by example, he encouraged his young sons to be among the satyagrahis from Peshawar. The leader of the 'Jatha' (group), which totalled about 2,500 volunteers, was Budh Dev Vidya Alankar, a famous Arya Samaj leader.

As the train was about to chug out of Peshawar station, Girdhari Lal stood there to flag off his sons. Girdhari Lal remained stoic as he saw them off. He was aware of the reports of harsh treatment being meted out to the satyagrahis in Hyderabad, yet he refused to let this affect his enthusiasm, or that of his sons. Brahm Dutt and Shiv Dutt, accompanied by other members of the group, were received at every station with warmth and love by enthusiastic supporters. After reaching Hyderabad, they marked their protest by displaying the book. This invited immediate action in the form of a lathi charge. They were arrested and jailed for six months. Out of the total 16,000 Hindus arrested from all over India by the Nizam of Hyderabad, 1200 were in one prison at Hyderabad Central Jail.

Girdhari Lal's sons were the youngest satyagrahis in the jail. Noting their youth, the police asked them to beg for clemency by admitting their mistake in joining the protesters. But they refused to do so, as their father had told them at the station not to ask for pardon in any situation if they believed their actions to be right. They would rather face death than go back after seeking an apology on such grounds. Finally, Shiv Dutt was released after three months due to the intense criticism by the press and pressure from the British Resident. Brahm Dutt was released only after six months. After their release, they lived in a camp for some time and returned to Lahore with a group of agitators who were released at the same time. Towards the middle of 1939, the Nizam of Hyderabad lifted the ban on *Satyartha Prakash* and the remaining satyagrahis were released from jail and returned to their homes.

Once the boys reached Peshawar, they were honoured with a grand reception. People praised them for their bold approach. But Girdhari Lal did not want to indulge in any form of self praise and felt that they had only performed their duty as nationalists. Nonetheless, this historic event became a turning point for him and his family. With this event, Girdhari Lal had established a name for himself and his family among the most politically influential. Girdhari Lal knew that people would expect a lot from him during these testing times and, in keeping with his earlier achievements, he was willing to live up to any challenge!

The Beginning of the Great Divide

The social and cultural developments in that era had a very strong correlation with the political scenario and it is important therefore to understand the latter. The NWFP was made up of six districts: Peshawar, Kouhat, Bannu, Dera Ismail Khan, Mardan and Abottabad. The Pathans of the area were a fiercely independent group. Hindus and Sikhs formed a small minority. But the Pathans were very secular and tolerant and there was no communal clash in the region. The elite Khan Pathans were close to the British and drew as much benefit from them as possible. The second rung of the Khans was anti-British and espoused the nationalist cause.

The Khudai Khidmatgar movement (Red Shirts), spearheaded by Khan Abdul Ghaffar Khan, was well organized and had close links with the larger freedom movement led by the Indian National Congress. The movement was formed on an ethnic and cultural basis and the Khidmatgars' basic demand was the autonomy of the region. They were proud of their Islamic identity but opposed the Muslim League and joined hands with the Congress. There were occasional skirmishes between the Pathans and the British. Beyond the five British agencies controlled by their political agents, the then Government of India did not interfere much in the peripheral areas of the province. The political agents controlled their respective areas through powerful landlords. The tribal areas, not under the control of the government, were again divided into several agencies in a similar manner.

The Reformists: Mahatma Gandhi with Khan Abdul Ghaffar Khan, leader of the Khudai Khidmatgar movement.

The main source of income for the people of these agencies was through the manufacture and sale of guns and drugs. In addition to the sales inflow, they would resort to looting and plunder to make ends meet. According to Maj Gen J.K. Kapoor (former student of Salwan Sanatan Dharam High School, Peshawar) they 'mostly looted Hindus by taking away money and sometimes took away their women. To attack people in

Peshawar, they would bring goons from elsewhere and kidnap people for ransom. The fortunate part, however, was that the wives and family members of the kidnappers looked after the kidnapped people. They were released once the ransom was paid. It was this system that Khan Abdul Ghaffar Khan tried to reform and he did succeed to a great extent.'

After the Second World War broke out, the communal harmony and peace that prevailed in the NWFP started showing signs of deterioration. In the 1937 elections, the Indian National Congress had swept the polls and formed governments in all provinces except the Punjab, Bengal and Sindh. Interestingly, out of the 482 seats reserved for the Muslims, the Muslim League (which claimed to represent the community) managed to win only a measly 108. In the NWFP, which had an overwhelming Muslim majority, the Muslim League did win a few seats. The defeat of the Muslim League resulted in bitter opposition to the Congress. The League's leaders tried to mislead the Muslim community by spreading the theory that the Muslim minority in India would be vulnerable.

The ongoing discord, hatred and animosity between the Hindus and the Muslims did not serve the interests of the British government, which was embroiled in the Second World War. At the 1940 Lahore Session, the Muslim League demanded a separate state of 'Pakistan'. The British, in a desperate bid for Indian support to the war efforts, tried to pacify the communal elements by sending Sir Stafford Cripps, who was known to be a radical leader and a supporter of the Indian national movement. Unfortunately, he formulated proposals which espoused the cause of the Muslim League and the creation of a separate Pakistan. The proposals emboldened the Muslim League and communal tension between the Muslims and the Hindus reached a crescendo. The violence that followed, spearheaded by zealots on both sides, led to death and destruction of a magnitude hitherto unknown in the history of the subcontinent.

The confusion that emerged in the wake of the creation of the two nations had not taken on a violent manifestation in NWFP. This was reinforced primarily due to the role of Khan Abdul Ghaffar Khan and his Khudai Khidmatgars. The influence of the Muslim League and radical clerics was minimal. Girdhari Lal, already perceived as a popular leader on account of his role in furthering education, took on the mantle of being the flag bearer for the minorities.

The first step that Girdhari Lal took was to strike a fine balance between two 'ideals'. He openly championed the minority cause and at the same time kept the doors of the schools open to all communities in accordance with his motto of 'Education for All.' He did not see any conflict of interest in this dual action, making this a shining example of how two right stances upon two independent philosophies can coexist without either one of them being termed wrong. Added to this, his focus on discipline and novel ways to instil confidence in the minority community by introducing physical exercise and a fitness regime worked wonders. Girdhari Lal converted a scared community into an integrated unit, physically responsive, mentally stronger and street-wise 'smarter'. Neither the Muslim League nor the radical clerics liked this one bit. The growing stature of Girdhari Lal was becoming difficult for them to handle.

As the demand for a separate Pakistan became louder, the resilience of the Pathans under Khan Abdul Ghaffar Khan became stronger, leading to unease in the NWFP. While the majority of Muslims rejected the demands of the Muslim League, they were simply outnumbered by the religious bigots who succeeded in spreading the communal venom everywhere.

Despite all the stratagems of the Muslim League, the Khudai Khidmatgars won the majority of Muslim seats. This gave them a clear majority in the provincial assembly, which meant a clear popular mandate against Partition. Though the Muslim League was routed, the party managed to win a few seats within the Pathan area. This, as stated by the historical facts, happened as a result of a conspiracy between the governor of the NWFP, Sir George Cunningham, and a section of the Muslim clerics. This blatant partisanship sponsored by the British prompted the badly defeated Muslim League to start a direct action demanding the dismissal of the democratically elected Congress government and imposition of governor's rule. They argued that in the changed political situation, the 1946 elections were no longer relevant and representative of popular opinion. It was against this backdrop that Girdhari Lal started mobilizing the minorities. The placid communal situation in the NWFP was thus being vitiated by the fundamentalists.

The Muslim League started treating the Hindus and the Sikhs as non-residents. Shiv Dutt recalls how they threatened the Hindu men and insulted and humiliated the women as well. Incidents of sporadic violence and murder of minorities became common. The age-old communal harmony was in jeopardy. The minorities, especially Hindus, were smaller in number but controlled businesses, professions and even bureaucratic cadres. The religious fundamentalism threatened the predominantly pluralistic complexion of the socio-cultural fabric. In fact, this was one of the key factors which irked the fundamentalists and ignited their envy.

Girdhari Lal was aware of all the happenings but wanted to remain aloof till matters settled down. Strategically he wanted to be in some kind of an official position to be able to leverage critical opinions and implement major decisions. He was seriously concerned about the indignities being heaped on the minorities. A point soon came when he could not stand it any longer. Shiv Dutt recalls, 'Next to Mehr Chand Khanna, he was the most prominent Hindu leader. While the former was the finance minister of the provincial government (which was headed by the Khudai Khidmatgar leader Dr Khan Sahib), my father was chosen president of Hindu organizations. As president, he was deeply involved in the peace-keeping activities, spearheading the interests of the Hindu and the Sikh minorities.'

Exponent of His Own Convictions

Despite the celebrated neutrality of the NWFP and its people, riots carried on almost unabated and the situation turned volatile. Tolerance levels fell on both sides, while Girdhari Lal comforted the minorities and inculcated in them a sense of self-protection. The thought process of Girdhari Lal was influenced by the ideals of the well-known socio-religious activist, Goswami Ganesh Dutt. A close associate of the Salwan family, Ganesh Dutt used to stay with them whenever he visited Peshawar. He would say, 'Never curse the darkness when you can light a lamp. Introspect and then you will be able to lighten the burdens of the tired, the wretched and the homeless.'

Elsewhere in the subcontinent, the Muslim League was gaining importance and was perceived by the Hindus as a major threat. This led to a rapid increase in the number of Hindus who joined the Rashtriya Swayamsevak Sangh (RSS). The common people found it difficult to differentiate between the Congress and the RSS when it came to the Muslim League's call for a separate state of Pakistan. The Hindus opposed this idea, but the Muslim fundamentalists persisted with their demands, creating insecurity for the Hindus. Girdhari Lal spearheaded their defence and fearlessly announced, 'As long as a single Hindu or Sikh breathes, we will not allow Pakistan to be created.' The Pathan community had no problem with the predominance of the Hindus in the socioeconomic field. A majority of them were anti-colonialist.

Well aware of the volatile situation, the government was examining all possibilities and measures to pre-empt further escalation of violence. At a meeting convened in Peshawar, the deputy commissioner urged the Hindus to dissolve the RSS, stating that otherwise the government would be compelled to ban the organization. Girdhari Lal had the courage to tell the deputy commissioner, 'Unless fundamentalist Muslim organizations like the Muslim National Guards are outlawed, there is no question of disbanding the RSS.' Bold statements of this nature provoked threats to the life of Girdhari Lal but he would always express himself frankly and fearlessly in accordance with his thoughts.

The strategy of the fundamentalists was to cause the maximum damage and target key people, like in their abortive attempt on the life of the educationist John Michael, who was a close friend of Girdhari Lal. As the main representative of the minorities in the NWFP, Girdhari Lal met Lord Mountbatten to oppose the partition of India. By this time, the Muslim League had declared that 16 August 1946 would be observed as 'Direct Action Day' for the creation of Pakistan. The situation eventually became uncontrollable.

Emergence of a Compassionate Leader in Turbulent Times

The communal strife suited the British strategy of 'divide and rule' and they subtly encouraged it. In the ensuing violence, women and children suffered the most. Kidnapping, arson and rapes were frequent. The Hindus and the Sikhs were aware of the plans of the Muslim League in Peshawar. It was a difficult experience for the families, who were torn by grief over the loss of their loved ones. How could they find consolation? Whom would they turn to in this hour of grief and insecurity? Where would they draw their strength from in order to go on affirming that life, love and faith are stronger than resignation, cynicism and death? During these testing times, Girdhari Lal stood by the people to reassure them and gave them strength to face the challenges ahead.

In remote villages, where the population of Hindus and Sikhs was miniscule, they were easy victims. To protect such people, Girdhari Lal helped in evacuating them and they were brought to the cities for safety. These refugees came in large numbers to Peshawar. Peshawar cantonment was safer than the surrounding areas, and every temple, gurdwara, school or any other Hindu or Sikh institution was converted into a refugee camp. He also threw open the doors of his own house for the refugees. They initially came for safety and then waited for evacuation. Shiv Dutt narrates this episode, 'When riots broke out, curfew was imposed in Peshawar. The scarcity of firewood forced my father to give away his furniture from the showroom to the needy, for cooking and other purposes. Despite the grim situation, people never thought that one day, they would have to leave the place. They could not imagine the partition of the country even in their wildest dreams.'

Sunset on Peshawar and Flight to Safety

During this time, the businessman in Girdhari Lal took a complete backseat, as the leader in him stood up for the safety and welfare of the people. He made frequent visits to Delhi to sensitize the Congress leadership to the security of minorities in the NWFP. His eldest son, Brahm Dutt, took over the business mantle. Brahm Dutt, twenty-three years old, was a good six feet, three inches tall, a strikingly handsome man with an affable temperament. He managed the business effectively.

It was destined that during one of Girdhari Lal's trips fate would strike a blow on the Salwan family. Girdhari Lal had gone to Delhi, along with Dev Prakash Shastri, to meet Sardar Patel and Pandit Nehru as part of a contingent comprising five prominent Hindu and Sikh representatives of Peshawar. The objective of the mission was to request air support for the evacuation of the refugees. People who had money and gold managed to get tickets and those who were not so privileged hoped to come out of Peshawar either by road or by train, though at the cost of grave risk as there had been numerous instances where trainloads of refugees were burnt to death. As Girdhari Lal was discussing the future of NWFP with Sardar Patel, the darkest moment for the Salwan family had already taken place back home in Peshawar.

Shiv Dutt closes his eyes, hiding his pain to narrate the following tale: 'The day was 27 August 1947. It was a regular day in the market, except for the fact that the atmosphere was charged and tense. Five men came into our showroom; they called Bhaisaab (Brahm Dutt) and started enquiring about the prices of the displayed furniture, posing as customers. He had

Brahm Dutt Salwan, eldest son of Girdhari Lal Salwan, became a victim of communal rage. He was murdered at the age of twenty-three in his own showroom in Peshawar in 1947.

no clue that they were not interested in furniture. Like a true businessman, he was involved in selling his wares. The next minute he was lying on the ground . . . those men had shot him. He was carried to the hospital by five RSS workers. On the way, two of the workers were also killed by the rioters. Bhaisaab braved all that and fought for his life valiantly. But he lost the battle a few hours before my father could reach from Delhi.'

In the cauldron of the national crisis, the sudden and cruel death of his eldest son was a major blow for Girdhari Lal. In just a fraction of a moment, he was transposed from the position of being a great son of the soil, to becoming the father of a martyr.

Shiv Dutt painfully relives those days: 'My father came on a special plane arranged by Sardar Patel. Curfew was imposed immediately. But it could not deter hundreds from paying their last homage to Brahm Dutt. My father was not allowed to attend the funeral by the government. I still remember the words "Hamla hoga inke upar" (He will be attacked).' The superintendent of the police told Girdhari Lal, 'Sahib, aapki jaan ko bahut khatra hai,' (Sir, your life is in danger) and so he was advised not to go to the cremation ground. 'I did the duties on his behalf.' Shiv Dutt says, 'It was discovered later that the Muslim fundamentalists had planned to kill him once he was out of the cremation ground.'

Brahm Dutt was survived by his wife Kaushalya Devi, a two-year-old son, Naresh Dutt, and a nine-month-old daughter, Shashi. The murder of his eldest son was a shock to Girdhari Lal but he took it very stoically and never allowed his personal grief to detract from his efforts towards helping others. His son was probably the first to be killed in Peshawar in such a gruesome manner.

The situation deteriorated further and by now intolerance and violence were prevalent in most parts of the NWFP. According to most residents, who later migrated to India, the Pathans were not involved in the violence against the minorities. No one felt threatened by them. Similarly, it was impossible to imagine that people would soon have to leave their homes and possessions and migrate to unfamiliar surroundings. Girdhari Lal's contribution in helping scores of such people cannot be expressed. He worked at great personal peril to help others. Here was a father who had lost his eldest son in communal frenzy, but he was not deterred from helping other hapless victims who had to cross the border to safety.

He continued to rescue, help and rehabilitate a number of women who were kidnapped during the communal violence. This was a very delicate issue and he wanted to entrust this work to someone he could rely on completely. So the baton was carried forward by his sister Parvati. She had ample experience of social service in Peshawar. At least 250 kidnapped women were rescued in this mission.

Following the murder of Brahm Dutt, Girdhari Lal, though unmindful of his personal safety, worked with greater zeal and determination than ever before. He would help anyone who was in need of evacuation. There was pressure on him from friends and well-wishers to leave Peshawar. But he refused, saying that he would leave Pakistan only after every Sikh and Hindu was evacuated to India. The Government of India, after the initial butchering of trainloads of refugees, sent Hindu and Sikh soldiers to accompany the refugees for safe transit to India. Everyone knew that there were people thirsty for his blood, but Girdhari Lal was adamant in his quest to remain in Peshawar and carry on with the task of evacuating as many people as possible.

It is said that an army officer who was involved in the rescue operations pleaded with him to leave, but he refused. The same officer threatened to kill himself if Girdhari Lal did not leave Peshawar. Finally, Girdhari Lal relented and listened to the voice of reason, bidding farewell to Peshawar, his house, his refugee camps and his schools.

The Persistence of Memory

Girdhari Lal's departure from Peshawar was a painful event. The man who had built everything from scratch had to leave everything behind. It was not just the monetary loss or material relinquishment that hit him. It was a feeling beyond that. It was the darkness that engulfs the soul when a person is forced to sever ties with the place he built with his own hands; the flourishing furniture business was mourned not for the commercial value but for the founder's emotive attachment to the wonderful works of art. Above all, what hurt him was leaving the soil upon which his father had stood, leaving behind a legacy. But he left with the promise of a new dawn, new challenges and new duties to be fulfilled on the other side of the border. The quest for life had to carry on as self-fulfilling prophecies moved towards the self actualization of Girdhari Lal.

But even though he moved on, Girdhari Lal's contributions to education and the socio-cultural field of Peshawar still stand tall. The Salwan School in Peshawar cantonment, which he built with his own hard-earned money, is still there with about 1000 students. The original signboards on the main entrance gate of the school at Sadar Bazar, Peshawar cantonment, are still visible.

Khan Faraz, former principal of Government Middle School, Peshawar cantonment (formerly known as Salwan Sanatan Dharam High School) in a letter written to Inder Dutt Salwan on 28 January 2001, says:

> I have been the principal of Salwan School, Peshawar Cantonment for the last twenty years. I am also the president of Pakistan Teachers' Organization Council and mine is the head office of the teachers' community of the country. All

Khan Faraz, who became principal of Salwan Sanatan Dharam High School after Girdhari Lal's departure from Peshawar, with Inder Dutt Salwan in 2001.

these credits go to your elder, Girdhari Lal Salwan, who had donated this historic building to the education sector as a tribute to the memory of his father, Mool Raj Salwan. The institution builder had perhaps an inner urge to build great hopes . . . and to carry out useful activities for the welfare of humanity. Politics or geography may change, but his history is eternal.

The bonds that students made with Girdhari Lal are so enduring and strong that one of the students of Salwan Sanatan Dharam High School, Peshawar, who retired as a brigadier from the Pakistan army, sent an email addressed to the Salwan Education Trust on 3 October 2011 stating, 'My name is Khalid Rashid. I belong to Peshawar. In fact, I was born there. You

Salwan Sanatan Dharam High School in Peshawar, now known as Government Middle School, Peshawar cantonment.

will be surprised to know that I was a student of Salwan School, Peshawar, during 1947-48. I still remember that it was the best school of the area. It was a brand new school in those days and had the best furniture. Hardly had I enjoyed the school for eight months when Partition took place.

'What a great visionary Girdhari Lal Salwan was. I salute him. I was further pleased to know there are eleven schools in India today in his name. Credit also goes to all the trustees and teachers who are carrying forward his mission. I, from across the border, wish you all the best and give you the good news that after sixty-four years his school is still intact and the mission, "Education for All" is continuing.'

The Educationist Rises Again

An Invocation

I thought that my voyage had come to its end
at the last limit of my power—
that the path before me was closed,
that provisions were exhausted and
the time come to take shelter in a silent obscurity.

But I find that thy will knows no end in me.
And when old words die out on the tongue,
new melodies break forth from the heart;
and where the old tracks are lost,
a new country is revealed with its wonders.

—Rabindranath Tagore
Gitanjali/Lyric 37

The Road to Delhi

It is impossible for those who did not live through it to comprehend the horror of Partition. The sights of drains running over with blood, of empty and burnt houses, scared faces, mourning eyes, shrieking shadows, rampaging mobs, and nightmare images of trainloads of dead bodies paints one of the most disturbing and gory portraits of human destruction in history.

Havelis were reduced to ruins and even those who had long been considered 'mighty' were vulnerable to the harsh tide of violence. People who had used coaches to travel and had lived in bungalows found themselves residents of refugee camps. Some of them reached either side of the newly minted border with nothing on their backs, not even a change of clothing. Many had lost their families and friends in the riots. A large number were separated from their family members. The search for even a temporary dwelling required more than the average level of fortitude and patience. So much had happened, so much had changed, that the people on either side of the border never imagined that they would find stability again.

The Government of India, though still in its infancy, was faced with a huge challenge: the resettlement of the refugees. The shortage of food, money and employment complicated the situation. Girdhari Lal, however, stood unfazed in the entire crisis. His resilience, his commitment towards society, was put to the ultimate test. The sorrow of leaving Peshawar, the wound of his son's death and the pain of separation from his schools were replaced by the urgency of the refugee situation. The magnitude of the national disaster mitigated his personal loss, rejuvenating the soul to live up to the challenge of the task ahead.

The 'mitti' of Delhi was destined to become the 'karambhoomi' of Girdhari Lal. The moment he landed at Delhi airport, the stage was set for the next lap of his eventful journey. The first help that came in his direction was a sum of Rs 10, 000 given by his brother-in-law, Diwan Chand Nabh, to enable him to begin the process of settling down. But driven by his selfless nature, he did not use the money which could have resettled him. Instead, he bought a jeep to ferry the refugees to various camps in Delhi from the airport and railway stations. Girdhari Lal worked zealously to help people who had come from Pakistan.

Be it the first ray of the morning sun or the darkest hour of the night, the needy always found Girdhari Lal waiting for them with his jeep. Arranging food for so many people was a major problem. The memory of the death of his son was still fresh in his mind. However, adversities did not deter him from continuing with what he had been doing in Peshawar. Hundreds had been living in his house in Peshawar before making the journey to India. So, for him the work among the refugees was just a continuation of the journey for community work. Only the geographical location had changed.

Girdhari Lal once again stood the test of time and worked relentlessly for the needy and to mitigate human suffering. He carried a dual responsibility towards society and towards his immediate family. His well-established business in Peshawar was a thing of the past. In Delhi he had come full circle, with nothing in his pocket. He had to start work all over again to establish himself in the community, providing a shoulder to the refugees and good education to the children.

Resettlement was not an easy task as communal unrest and the riots would raise their ugly head intermittently. If on one hand there was Girdhari Lal braving all odds, on the other there was the constant threat of riots in Delhi. Meanwhile, the political stage remained vibrant with a series of fast-paced developments. Gandhiji had gone on a fast against the riots. Shiv Dutt Salwan remembers vividly, 'My father and his companions asked Gandhiji why he never fasted to protest against the riots in Punjab and other places in the newly-created Pakistan but only against riots in Calcutta and Delhi.' They wanted to know why, after Partition, nothing was being done about those who were forced to leave everything in Pakistan and escape to India? Where would they go? What would they do?

He recalls: 'When my father voiced his opinion, Gandhiji replied, "Aap sab sharanarthi hain" (You are refugees). Then my father retorted, "Hum sharan mein nahin aaye hain, hum toh apnee zimewariyan sambhalne ayayee hain". (We haven't come as mere refugees, we have come to shoulder our responsibilities).'

While Girdhari Lal provided sustained support for the cause of the refugees, in principle he did not support the concept of 'partial' migration of the population on religious grounds as propagated by Gandhiji, with the backing of Pandit Nehru. Rehabilitation was a gigantic task involving thousands of people spread over a huge number of camps. Monetary assistance too was a pressing need to bring some form of relief to the affected people. The Government of India formed four committees for the rehabilitation of the refugees. Ajit Prasad Jain was the rehabilitation minister with Mehr Chand Khanna as the advisor. The ministry had drawn up certain criteria for providing monetary help to each family, ranging from Rs 50 to Rs 250 per month and, in some cases, Rs 500. The distribution of work was entrusted to officials who came from different parts of India, serving the Central government. Given their background, the process was slow as they looked upon the problem with a bureaucratic mindset. Most of the refugees had no papers to prove their antecedents in Pakistan. They would say that they had a house, business or job but there were no records to support their claims.

Consequently the officials who handled this issue could not really support the refugees though they were desirous of helping them. The solution required someone who could understand and relate with those helpless victims of the political turmoil. For handling the cases of people from the NWFP, Mehr Chand Khanna earmarked Girdhari Lal, as he knew his abilities and had trust in him.

After taking charge of the refugees from the NWFP area, Girdhari Lal adopted a humanitarian approach backed by common sense. He would call and interview the refugees. If someone had valid documents, it was easy; otherwise he would ask the person to get someone else to testify about his antecedents. Once he was convinced about the veracity of the claims, Girdhari Lal would recommend the amount of financial aid as per the guidelines. He knew that some of them had enjoyed a very high standard of living in Pakistan and had palatial houses. It was cruel to give such people Rs 50 or Rs 100 per month. After due verification and satisfaction on the authenticity of the claim, he would recommend the maximum possible monthly allowance. These families were rehabilitated in the hostile rocky terrain of Rajendra Nagar on the outskirts of Delhi.

The question of earning one's bread, no doubt, was important, but more important was the need to build a future to become self-reliant. According to Shiv Dutt, who was personally involved at all stages, 'Every person from the NWFP started getting the financial allowance from the government in a month's time. The story of people who came from elsewhere, like Quetta, Baluchistan or Punjab or Sindh, was different. In their case, the processing went on and on and in certain cases, it took years. Ultimately the government abolished that system.'

Trilochan Singh, a young Congress leader from Peshawar who worked for the rehabilitation of the uprooted, recalls, 'When we came over to Delhi, Pandit Salwan and I became closer, primarily because we were both involved in the rehabilitation work. In fact, he was playing a very important, dynamic and a more constructive role, whereas I was involved in the political side of rehabilitation. He was doing a great job by approaching the government, asking for land for building colonies, providing loans and other kinds of assistance. I was living in Paharganj; Pandit Salwan too was residing there. He owned a furniture workshop. His showroom was in Connaught Place and my main area of activity was also in the same area. His showroom used to be our meeting place. I often met him at his workshop in the morning. He was always occupied, giving instructions and overseeing the work of his carpenters.'

Trilochan Singh continues: 'He was very clear that he must have financial and economic independence so that he would have the strength to fight or raise issues. He had tremendous help from Mehr Chand Khanna who had also migrated to Delhi. To begin with, he was appointed advisor to the rehabilitation ministry, which had Ajit Prasad Jain as minister. Shri Salwan and I used to meet at Mehr Chand Khanna's house almost every day. There were some organizations of refugees in which we were both involved. I was on the committee of the Custodians of Evacuee Property and Uma Shankar Dikshit, who later became the home minister, was also a custodian. The custodians looked after all the properties left by those who had migrated to Pakistan. I remember that this project of the school was conceived, and of course it was primarily Girdhari Lal's idea. He had carried in his heart the same passion which he had in Peshawar.'

Rajendra Nagar, the New Home for Refugees

The rocky area called Rajendra Nagar was like the Promised Land for many a soul. This resettlement colony was named after the first president of India, Dr Rajendra Prasad. People were living in tents on a monthly allowance, and had many mouths to feed. Some were living with their relatives. Many homes had hundreds of people living and dining together. They were sort of community kitchens, rather than family dwellings, where just enough 'chapattis' and 'daal' were available. The people who were able to cross the border had developed a strong sense of resilience but the fact remained that every family needed a place to stay. Girdhari Lal worked with Mehr Chand Khanna and others to build houses for the refugees.

After a great deal of persuasion, the government 'subsidized' houses, and allotted them to people from the NWFP and West

Punjab and Sind. There were two types of plots: 50 yards and 88 yards. Each house was offered for either Rs 19 per month for a number of years or a lump sum of Rs 4600 for the bigger and Rs 3200 for the smaller plots. For a large number of refugees, even these amounts were much beyond their capacity as some of them had no money at all.

Houses built with bricks and asbestos sheets and providing for basic needs were the definition of luxury for those who had long lived in tents. The Rajendra Nagar colony lacked proper infrastructure and even the basic amenities were inadequate. The fortunate ones among the refugees could get some employment. Some others, who were basically from a business background, started petty businesses. The urge to rebuild their devastated lives was very strong. There was no time for false prestige and living in the glory of the past. Some people would walk for miles to find a job. Sometimes a relation considered lost or killed in the riots would suddenly reappear. Food and security remained a common priority. Everything else could wait. The people had indomitable courage and a rare instinct for survival. Yet the situation in the resettlement colonies was depressing. Men and women sitting quietly in corners, gazing into the distance, were a common sight. Dreams of new lives and careers had been shattered. Many had escaped from the jaws of death with empty pockets and no papers to prove their antecedents. Depression was writ large on many faces.

The rocky area was turning out to be a haven for many as petty businesses linked to groceries and eateries started supporting the commune, besides being a source of income for the promoters. The Rajendra Nagar of those days was a far cry from the developed place it is today. There were tents all around with a few hutments coming up. There was no proper transport. People carried water from the market place. The lampposts were the only landmark.

Spreading the Light of Knowledge:
Educate the Child, Build a Nation

While people were slowly settling down and getting used to the surroundings, education for the children remained a major concern. There was only one small school in the Rajendra Nagar area named Amar Vidyalaya. This school was run and managed by a mendicant called Swamiji in three refugee quarters. For the children of this resettlement colony, the school was a boon; only a few parents could afford to send their children to schools far away from the central area. The others had no alternative, even though the children were crammed in small rooms in Amar Vidyalaya during the unbearable heat of the Delhi summer. Girdhari Lal was aware of the need and also conscious of the fact that short-term quick-fix solutions would not work. Undeterred by the multiple obstacles this endeavour promised to hold, he embarked upon the path to spread education to the masses. Equipped with first-hand experience from the Peshawar school, he started strategizing for the project.

He considered education the most important element in a child's growth, and integral to the fulfilment of his own cherished ideal of national integration. He always emphasized: 'The soul of a nation is its people; people who so implicitly and reflexively weave their lives around their nation, and when the soul is enslaved, how can the body be free? This is the eternal promise of national integration.' Despite his commitment to the cause of education, Girdhari Lal failed to get a head start with any project on account of the economic constraints in the aftermath of the Partition and nobody was prepared to build a school. The government had other priorities and was not in a position to focus on the school project. Despite the setback, Girdhari Lal's interest in education remained deep-rooted. His friend and well-wisher Mehr Chand Khanna and others were also eager to help him in getting land for a school and they kept hope alive through their parleys with the government. Finally, the land for a school was allotted in 1948.

Rehabilitation of the Family and Business

Girdhari Lal was now sharing the responsibility of his fellow beings from the NWFP and whatever time he had was devoted to his family. They settled in the congested area of Paharganj, where Girdhari Lal was allotted a workshop for his furniture business. The business was re-established in the year 1949.

According to Shiv Dutt, his father constructed a temporary building in a 'kabristan' (graveyard) which was behind the Public Works Department (PWD) quarters in Paharganj. They lived under such arrangements till 1952. The family moved to a new plot on Pusa Road and initially stayed in tents. Later, the house was constructed. In lieu of his furniture shop in Peshawar, he was allotted a place on a rental basis in the Marina Arcade complex at Connaught Circus. The tenant of the shop had migrated to Pakistan and the property was declared an evacuee property. Shiv Dutt recalls, 'As there was no electricity and water connection on the Pusa Road premises,

Panditji used to have his bath and get dressed at the furniture showroom in Marina Arcade.'

The Salwans had property worth more than Rs 50 lakh in Peshawar at that time. But the compensation received from the government was just Rs 2 lakh as per the upper limit. Even this compensation amount was used to adjust the loans taken from the rehabilitation ministry for the business and for the residential plot on Pusa Road. Salwan Furniture soon became famous for the quality products it manufactured. The refugee community came to trust the man for his work once again. His sons, Shiv Dutt and Ramesh Dutt, gave him a helping hand by devoting all their time to the business and thereby giving their father sufficient time in his work of supporting the community.

The First Salwan School

At this point of time, establishment of educational institutions was the uppermost task and not the rehabilitation of the self. The first Boys and Girls schools were started in tents. Salwan Boys School had over 3000 students working in two shifts. The morning shift was for girls and the evening shift for boys. Girdhari Lal once again began his tireless quest to find capable teachers. His work was rewarded when many of his old teachers, like Master Hari Ram, Master Shiv Ram, Master Lorinda Mal and Dev Prakash Shastri joined him.

The Salwan Boys School building was completed in four months with the Salwan Girls School building coming up in six months. Adjacent to the school buildings in Rajendra Nagar was a four-acre plot of land. As the Salwan Schools had no playground, Girdhari Lal applied for that land.

He felt that for a school, a playground is a must and unless children are initiated into playing games in the field, how could a nation of strong youth be built? Adversities were Girdhari Lal's constant companions. Considering that he always fought for the welfare of others, it was ironic to see him fighting his battles all alone. Immediately after the land for the school was acquired and construction had started, there was opposition. Shiv Dutt recalls, 'There were many rounds of agitations by the residents. Most of the people who were allotted the residential quarters in Rajendra Nagar were influential in their own way and were dead set against the allotment of the playground for the school though their own children were studying in the school. They wanted to use the land to organize public functions, like Dussehra etc.'

Shiv Dutt continues, 'So for one or two years, there was an agitation every day. We would build the gate in the day time and they demolished the same in the night . . . so ultimately with great difficulty, persuasion and threats, my father said, "Nothing doing. I am not doing it for myself. Your children are the beneficiaries, ask your children whether they want to play or not," as he was of the opinion that unless there is a playground for the students, they can't develop their mental faculties. Soon the issue was resolved and the playground came up.'

As part of the development initiative, seven acres of additional land was allotted to the Salwan Education Trust. Then there were two tracks of open land between the park and the side of the Boys and the Girls school. This was a security risk. On representation, those tracks were also sold to the Trust by the government and integrated into the master plan for the complex. Later on, the government also gave more land for a nursery school to the Trust and another piece of land for educational activities, thereby making it the biggest campus of the Salwan Schools in Delhi. Today, the campus stands on a twelve-acre plot.

Re-establishing the Salwan Education Trust

After Partition, the Salwan Education Trust was re-established in 1950 as a registered charitable society. It was registered under the certificate of Registration of Societies Act XXI of 1860. The members were people of eminence in public life, experts in their respective fields who contributed greatly to the founder's vision. Girdhari Lal was aware that the daunting task of providing education for all could not be undertaken single-handedly and therefore he had gathered the aid and support of like-minded and progressive people like Mehr Chand Khanna and Dharam Vira, former governor of West Bengal, to help him convert his vision into reality. The Salwan Education Trust was registered on 30 March 1950 with the following members:

- Girdhari Lal Salwan   Chairman
- Deshbandhu Gupta   Vice President
- Lala Hans Raj Gupta   Vice Chairman
- Rai Bahadur Dina Nath   Member
- Uttam Singh Dugal   Member
- Rai Sahib Roora Ram   Member
- Mallick Nanak Chand   Member
- Sardar Babek Singh   Member
- Fakir Chand Marwah   Secretary and Treasurer
- Purshottam Dutta   Assistant Secretary

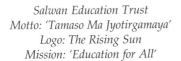

Salwan Education Trust
Motto: 'Tamaso Ma Jyotirgamaya'
Logo: The Rising Sun
Mission: 'Education for All'

Salwan Public School
Motto: 'Service Before Self'
Logo: The Rising Sun

The motto 'Tamaso Ma Jyotirgamaya,' which is inscribed on the crest of the Salwan Education Trust, forms the second mantra of the Brihadaranyaka Upanishad (I.iii.28). In the literal sense it means 'Lead us from darkness to light.' The only remedy for darkness is light; the only remedy for ignorance is knowledge.

The logo depicting the rising sun is a manifestation of the mission of 'Service before Self.' It reflects a commitment to serve others willingly, graciously and selflessly. It represents the Salwan Education Trust's (SET's) objectives and its multi-dimensional efforts to spread the light of knowledge and selfless service to society. It envisages the holistic growth of everyone commencing with the educational dimension and extending to every sphere and section of society. The emphasis is on the need to strive hard to rejuvenate and invigorate the educational spirit in a manner relevant to the contemporary scenario.

The members of the Trust were active participants in the functioning of the Trust. They were also seen at major programmes of the school. Their suggestions were taken seriously when it came to managing the affairs of the schools. The traditions established by the founder became the essence for the future generations.

The late Fakir Chand Marwah used to recall: 'I appreciated Girdhari Lal for his enthusiasm. Salwan Sahib and I managed the school which was initially in tents but soon the "pucca" buildings came up. There were good lawns. Girdhari Lal Salwan took personal care of the lawns; even if someone plucked a flower he would come to know who did it. He was a strong and sturdy gentleman who looked after the construction and maintenance of the schools. The Boys and the Girls Schools were entirely his effort. He would work for the whole day and then prepare a blueprint for the future. He had the urge to develop not only in the physical sense, but also in terms of propagating ideas and carrying out useful activities for the welfare of humanity, for which he worked throughout his life.'

One can witness the results of the exemplary vision of the Salwan Education Trust in the excellent infrastructural facilities it has created for the multidimensional progress of Salwanians.

Salwan Boys Senior Secondary School

The school was started on 9 September 1949. Dina Nath Datta, who became the first principal of the Salwan Boys School, narrates his own story: 'I came to Delhi after Partition. I worked in M.B. Higher Secondary School in Gole Market.

When this school started, I was introduced by one of my old students to Mohan Lal Saxena (rehabilitation minister). He enquired whether I knew Salwan Sahib. I told him that I had heard of him as a good man, desirous of spreading education, because he himself was almost uneducated; but he had all the skills and talent in him to run a school . . . He depended on me and I depended on him. Salwan was a sturdy and strong gentleman.'

Dr Rajendra Prasad visited the school in 1953 and showered his praise upon it, saying:

Independent India's first president, Dr Rajendra Prasad, visited Salwan Boys School in 1953. Second and third from the right are Mehr Chand Khanna, advisor to the rehabilitation ministry, and Girdhari Lal Salwan.

The great work that Salwan Sahib has done in the cause of education has made me very happy. This monumental work will confer immortality on him.

Deshbandhu Chawla (a former student) recalls the science exhibition organized at the inter-school level: 'When I was in class VIII, I assembled a radio set, which was to be displayed by the organizers of the science exhibition. Questioning a class VIII student's ability to assemble a radio set, the organizers never displayed mine. I was very disappointed. Then our principal, D.N. Datta, displayed my radio too in the school assembly and encouraged me. The whole school applauded me.'

During Ram Lila, there used to be a big mela in the Salwan compound. People used to come in large numbers from

Salwan Boys School in Rajendra Nagar, New Delhi, 1949. Girdhari Lal built the school from scratch on a rocky, barren piece of land in a record time of four months.

Pandit Jawaharlal Nehru, Indira Gandhi and foreign delegates when they visited the school. On the extreme right is J.R. Mullick, the manager of the school.

Rajendra Nagar, Patel Nagar and Pusa Institute to see the huge effigy of Ravana burning. 'All the arrangements for the "Ravan Dahan" were made by Salwan Sahib, who bore all the expenses,' recalls Yash Oberoi (a former student).

Salwan Girls Senior Secondary School

Rajni Kumar, the chairperson of Springdales Education Society, Delhi, has fond memories of the early days of the school. As the initiator of the Girls school she was a witness to those exciting years of birth and growth and the challenges met and coped with. She states, 'I saw the advertisement in the paper, applied for the post and was called for an interview before the Trust. This was the first time I had set eyes on Girdhari Lal Salwan, the chairperson of the Trust. He was dressed in a light brown shirt and trousers, he had a sturdy physique and a determined look on his face. He was watching me intently throughout the interview, absorbing everything, but saying little, but I knew that in his mind, I was the candidate of his choice. Some of the people sitting with him on the interviewing board were wearing the typical Frontier dress with impressive headgear (one of them was Fakir Chand Marwah, the manager of the schools). Maybe the chairman was not a product of an English-oriented education system but he was a man with vision; a great builder, designer and creator with tremendous reserves of energy, drive and the capacity to turn his dreams and visions into reality.'

Rajni Kumar continues, 'He brushed aside all arguments put forward by the Trust, which stated that I was only twenty-six years old and too young and inexperienced for the job, and that I knew little about Indian culture and language. He put his trust in me, told me that I could have a free hand in building up the school, and that all he looked for was the result. I realized that it was a big challenge for me.'

The Girls School was inaugurated by Ajit Prasad Jain (former rehabilitation minister) in 1952. He said:

> Salwan Sahib has a marvellous ability for work. Establishing two great institutions within the span of a year is no less than magical. He has done the refugee boys and girls a great favour by starting these schools and catering to their educational needs.

The furniture for the classrooms was sparse and there was hardly any teaching apparatus, except for blackboards, chalk, mats and chairs for the children. The important thing was that there was a commitment towards everything and as part of the development process some matters were more imperative and given a higher priority than others. It was obvious that getting the correct human resource was the most critical factor. The management was able to get together a really fine team of teachers, devoted to the cause of education and knowledgeable in their subjects. Nearly all of them were displaced persons themselves and some had taken part in the freedom movement. They had the spirit and the urge to help in the development of the country.

Pandit Jawaharlal Nehru with Sushila Nayyar, Ajit Prasad Jain (to Nehru's right) and Girdhari Lal Salwan (to Nehru's left) at the Salwan Boys School.

A.S. Chaudhary, who lives in the immediate neighbourhood of the school, says: 'Once when I came down from the hostel, my uncle asked me whether I wanted to see a movie in Salwan School. It was *Baiju Bawra*. Girdhari Lalji and his associate

Pandit Jawharlal Nehru taking the salute from a marching contingent of the Salwan Girls School.

Students of Salwan Girls Senior Secondary School interact with Pandit Nehru in Rajendra Nagar.

were collecting five annas. I asked Girdhari Lalji, "Uncle ji aap ko paise ki kya kami hain? Aap ke pass toh itne paise hain, aapko yeh karneki kya zaroorat hai?" (Uncle ji, you are not short of money. You have a lot of money. There is no need for you to do all this.) He replied: "Beta yeh paisa mere liye nahin hai; yeh school bananey ke liye hai." (Son, this money is not for me. It is for the construction of the school.) I used to see him working day in and day out. Finally he was able to make a great success of this school. I remember when he died, there were thousands of people at his funeral.'

Another dignitary who visited the Salwan campus was General (later Field Marshal) K.M. Cariappa, who assumed office as the first commander-in-chief of the Indian Army in 1949.

Pandit Nehru and other dignitaries inspecting the swimming pool at Salwan Boys Senior Secondary School in Rajendra Nagar.

General Cariappa on a school visit with (from left to right) Principal Dina Nath Datta, Trilochan Singh, Girdhari Lal Salwan, Fakir Chand Marwah and Rajni Kumar.

In the year 1953, the Indian Education Commission for Secondary Education under the chairmanship of Dr Ramaswamy Mudaliar visited the school. The school was especially chosen for this visit because of the innovations and good practices it had introduced at the secondary level and the aesthetically constructed building and pleasing learning environment.

Rajni Kumar recalls: 'As the school was imparting education to girls from class VI onwards, I suggested to Shri Salwan that we could start a kindergarten school on Montessori lines to give a good start in life to children at pre-school level. It would also be a self-supporting unit. He responded warmly to the idea and allocated a wing in the building for the tiny tots.'

Kumar adds: 'Much of my success in building Springdales was due to the lessons I learnt at Salwan School; to value the human resource that forms the base of good education; to realize that there is potential in every child which can be brought out if the opportunity is given; that to achieve our goals we need to work with passion and energy; that we must be strong in confronting problems and to follow the dictates of our conscience fearlessly, regardless of the fruits of our actions or the pain it might bring. It was a training ground for me and a true learning experience. Shri G.L. Salwan was a great pioneer and made a very rich contribution to the cause of education by giving opportunities to thousands of children to learn and grow at a time when it was desperately needed. Personalities come and go but rarely do they leave behind

Girdhari Lal Salwan (centre) with the chief commissioner of Delhi, A.D. Pandit (on his left), and Rajni Kumar (on his right), shares a light moment with members of the staff and students.

footprints in the sands of time as Salwan has done. The schools he created stand on firm and strong foundations today, as monuments to his pioneering spirit and creative genius. Sixty years on, I pay my humble tribute to his memory.'

The former prime minister of Pakistan, Janab Mohammed Ali Bogra, and his wife brought back memories from Peshawar as they visited the Salwan School in New Delhi.

It was a great occasion when a dignitary of special eminence visited the Salwan Schools at the Rajendra Nagar campus. Janab Mohammed Ali Bogra, the former prime minister of Pakistan, was personally received by Girdhari Lal and escorted to all the facilities in the school. This was a special occasion for Girdhari Lal as Bogra represented the country where Girdhari Lal had made a humble beginning and the visit triggered fond memories of the institutions at Peshawar. After seeing the

Salwan institutions, Bogra remarked:

> I am returning to Pakistan with a new hope and will. They [the schools] are eloquent testimonials to Girdhari Lal's unique courage and firm determination. He has shown a path that, if followed by all on this subcontinent, can lead to happiness and prosperity.

Kailashnath Katju, the Union home minister, was the chief guest for the annual Sports Day of the Girls School in 1953. He thoroughly enjoyed the qawwali that the students sang in Hindustani, lamenting their sad plight at having to study so hard and wishing that every day would be a Tuesday, the Hindu holy day!

Kailashnath Katju, the Union home minister, addresses the students at Salwan Girls School, 1953.

Katju said:

> I have been to many countries and have seen many educational
> institutions. The Salwan institutions rank among the best in
> the world so far as the discipline, facilities and grandness are
> concerned. The founder of those institutions, Girdhari Lal
> Salwan, deserves all praise. Posterity will remember him as
> 'Salwan the Great'.

The Documentary Films of India presentation *Nai Bastiyan*
transports the viewer to the stark realities of the aftermath of
the Partition of India. The human instinct for survival, the
spirit of resilience and the will to eke an earning out of
practically nothing is the leitmotif of Girdhari Lal Salwan's
life.

Salwan Montessori School, Rajendra Nagar

Initially, the Salwan Montessori plot was allotted for the
construction of an industrial and Montessori School. The
Japanese government gave machines for the skill-training of
refugees. But as there were no schools in and around Rajendra
Nagar, there was a need for the foundation of a good public
school.

In 1952 the Salwan Montessori School joined the growing
community of schools at the common infrastructure of
Rajendra Nagar, providing a wide spectrum of educational
possibilities. By now even the education department was fairly
open to providing grants and approvals for infrastructure and
development, recognizing the long-term commitment of the
Trust towards the cause of 'Education for All'.

The foundation stone of Salwan Industrial and Montessori School was laid by Shankar Prasad, ICS, former chief commissioner of Delhi (right), in 1952.

Salwan Public School, Rajendra Nagar

Girdhari Lal had a lot of followers and a large enough network of associates but his immediate inner circle of friends was very small. However, it formed a repository of intelligence and vision, providing him with support and inspiration in his mission.

In 1953, an important interaction with an old friend sowed the seeds of yet another idea. John Michael, principal of St. John's School in Peshawar, shared an intense bond with Girdhari Lal. They shared and discussed aspects of imparting education through innovative approaches during their countless evening strolls. Those sessions had often proved to be eye-openers for Girdhari Lal. During Partition, John Michael had moved to south India. The separation failed to divide their hearts. In fact, Girdhari Lal named one of his grandsons Micheal. Michael's visit to Delhi became an occasion to celebrate the old association. The reunion was emotional, showcasing that true friendship is beyond riches and titles. Michael was very pleased to see that his old friend's strong sense of commitment to the cause of education was undeterred by the passage of time.

John Michael's tour of the Rajendra Nagar campus and the sight of the schools overwhelmed him. He voiced his feelings thus: 'Imparting knowledge and values with full earnestness is the greatest service any person can render to an individual, society and nation. I greatly admire Salwan's boundless enthusiasm, human enterprise, perseverance, exemplary ethics and profound compassion for the vital cause. It is indeed heartening to see that his establishments are acting as true catalysts and spreading the essence of his ideals to everyone. I sincerely wish that the country's long journey towards educational growth, so dear to him, is achieved.'

Girdhari Lal and John Michael resumed their evening routine, picking up the threads from where they had left them in the past, discussing various issues amongst which the problem of running aided schools surfaced. Matters pertaining to funds for paying the teaching and non-teaching staff and maintaining the school buildings were also discussed; as also the fact that Girdhari Lal had exhausted all his resources in building the schools. There was already tension among teachers for not being paid on time and this was threatening to reach a breaking point. Michael listened patiently to everything and instantly understood and related to Girdhari Lal's problems.

Both Salwan Boys and Girls schools were Hindi medium schools and education was absolutely free.

He suggested that Girdhari Lal start an English medium school immediately where fees could be charged. The savings from the English medium school could help the management to run the aided schools.

Such a pragmatic suggestion by a seasoned and trusted friend made sense. Unlike today, in those days there was no decent English medium school in Rajendra Nagar or adjoining areas. The basic infrastructure of the school was built very fast and in 1953, the Salwan Public School was inaugurated. Standing in front of the new building in Rajendra Nagar, Girdhari Lal beamed with pride and satisfaction.

The school soon became a revered temple of learning. Based on the holistic approach, its task was cut out to help students harness their full potential. Guided by such an immaculate vision and focused mission, the school established itself in a league of its own. Though all the schools so far had created unique positions on the ever growing Salwan campus, there is no denying the fact that the year 1953 proved to be a landmark in the establishment of a common education hub at the campus with the addition of Salwan Public School.

G.C. Sharma, who was the first principal of the Salwan Public School and a close associate of Girdhari Lal, remembers him as a man of great commitment and discipline. 'We (the principals) enjoyed freedom as long as we were instrumental in moving the school in the right direction. On all occasions Salwan would keep to the background and would rarely come forward for photographs or interactions, though he was always there to see that everything went off in style and with clock-like precision, overseeing every detail of what was going on.'

Girdhari Lal—The Architect

The land allotted for the schools was barren and rocky. It was Girdhari Lal's tireless efforts that made the land fit to house a school complex. He personally supervised the construction site and stayed there from early morning till late evening, giving instructions and supervising work. He would not tolerate any bad or substandard construction. His close monitoring was so effective that there was no question of any patchwork or repair. He got timely support from Krishan Salwan, a close member of the Salwan family, who officiated as a manager and provided pivotal support for the completion of the projects.

Dr H.J. Chibber (former student of the Salwan Girls School) recalls: 'I remember one thing; they were building the verandah of the Boys School and we were playing around there. Suddenly, we heard a deafening sound. The roofs of 10-15 columns of the veranda came down, because he (Girdhari Lal) pulled them down as one or two were not aligned properly. People normally demolish the ones which are not aligned, but Shri Salwan said they all had to be in order. He was very particular about the precision. He was a very impressive figure though he was not very educated. But he would roam around in the campus like a "sher" (lion)! He would check everything to see whether things were done properly or not!'

Trilochan Singh, who became trustee of the school for some years, remembers Girdhari Lal as an institution builder with single-minded devotion. He recalls: 'The construction or building of the schools revealed that he was a multi-faceted person. For instance, he even designed buildings himself, maybe with the help of architects. Even in the construction, he was all the time at the site, personally directing, guiding, and overseeing the construction. He was even there in the laying down of the ground or grass courts or flower beds. Same thing goes for designing the equipment and furnishings. That showed that he had tremendous potential. He was a practical person in the real sense.'

Girdhari Lal was full of creative ideas that could easily be channelized through the furniture business. Like education, the vocation of fabrication and construction too was followed with a holistic approach. He observed and analyzed the impact of the elements like wind, rain and sun on wood and civic structures. He would work at the layout and plan, including basic raw material, in accordance with tropical climates and the changing seasons. Right from the first brick at Salwan Sanatan Dharam High School at Peshawar to the Salwan Public School at New Delhi, the handiwork of a man with an eye for design and detail is evident in the exteriors and the interiors of the institutes. What is remarkable is the use of local material to conceptualize, plan and systematically convert his ideas into reality. The wide verandahs outside the classrooms, big windows and ventilators for cross-ventilation were structured to ensure that the school premises were cool in the summers.

Gearing Up for Challenges Ahead

Girdhari Lal was a man gifted with a unique and strong-willed determination to fight against all odds. He had mastered the art of construction and had an outstanding vision of holistic education, encompassing extracurricular activities. Girdhari Lal used to get the best out of people by leading from the front. The manner in which he went about the mission of

'Education for All' was like an unquenchable thirst to fill the 'education' void within him.

It is said that even the river that flows on a predetermined track, well rehearsed for decades and centuries, at times changes track due to forces beyond its control. These changes are generally attributed to man-made causes and actions undertaken for personal gain and are not really considered natural circumstances. It is also said that when others intervene with corrective steps, the river once again changes course and gets back to the original path. Similarly, the life and times of Girdhari Lal were made to change course circumstantially and return to the mainstream once the aberration was dealt with. This aberration was a deviation necessitated by compelling circumstances brought up in the interest of the schools but viewed through legal eyes as a criminal deviation that had to be dealt with. Fighting the forces of adversity with moral courage was by now second nature for Girdhari Lal and so this too was part of his struggle.

The Years of Struggle

An Invocation

Clouds heap upon clouds and it darkens.
Ah, love, why dost thou let me wait
outside at the door all alone?

In the busy moments of the noontide work
I am with the crowd, but on this dark lonely day
it is only for thee that I hope.

If thou showest me not thy face, if thou leavest me
wholly aside, I know not how I am to pass these
long, rainy hours.

I keep gazing on the far-away gloom of the sky,
and my heart wanders wailing with the restless wind.

—Rabindranath Tagore
Gitanjali/Lyric 18

Facts and Circumstances

The schools were running smoothly. The school buildings and grounds were well laid and impressive. Three schools—the Boys, the Girls and the Montessori School—had been established. A considerable number of refugee teachers had been employed and there were also considerable employment opportunities for disabled persons. However, there was latent discontent amongst the staff owing to irregular and delayed payment of salaries. This came to the fore and took on an ugly turn in March 1954.

Ram Swaroop, a teacher in the school, was found guilty by the management for leaking an examination question paper to his class. He made a veiled confession of his guilt. On compassionate grounds, the Trust, instead of dismissing him, gave a lenient punishment, but later on, changed its mind and passed an order of dismissal. This order was received by the Department of Education and the punishment originally awarded was modified, the dismissal order was set aside and the teacher was ordered to be reinstated. The Trust did not accept this order, which caused some insecurity to the staff. This resulted in some resentment among the staff. The other issue came up in the Girls School, where Rajni Kumar tendered her resignation and submitted a number of complaints. In view of her complaints not being settled, she drew the attention of the Department of Education. In the meantime, her resignation was accepted, but the department asked her to continue. Thus arose a tense atmosphere and later, a strike.

A number of complaints had been made against Girdhari Lal Salwan and the government had asked Mr Goyal, a magistrate, to enquire into these complaints. He made a full report to the government on all these matters. Enquiries were also made by the Department of Education about irregular accounts and misuse of funds by the Trustees and it solicited a report for the same. During all these enquiries, a tense atmosphere existed among the residents and in the schools and a good deal of agitation was launched against Girdhari Lal.

The dispute was referred by the then chief minister of Delhi, Gurmukh Nihal Singh (who had taken over the portfolio of education) for arbitration to Justice Mehr Chand Mahajan, former chief justice of India.

After years of hard work, Girdhari Lal was faced with a public questioning of his integrity, dignity and the worth of his mission. But finally this was the award for Salwan Schools announced by Justice Mahajan on 19 April 1955:

> It is a matter of great credit that Shri Salwan, being himself a refugee, has by his individual effort and out of his own private resources along with government aid built this fine institution which may well be the envy of other schools in Delhi. By this munificence he has arranged for the education of thousands of children and has provided employment for a considerable number of refugee teachers and others. I feel people should be grateful to him for what he has done.
>
> Though Shri Salwan is a great builder and is a resourceful personality and a fighter as well, he is, all said and done, a poor manager of educational institutions. Being a man from the north, he has a rough exterior and manners which are in sharp contrast to the climate and mannerisms of metropolitan India and these factors have, to a certain extent, made him unpopular with a faction of the staff, the principals and certain people in the locality.
>
> The schools and the Trust had no financial backing from the

very start. The Trust, when it was registered as a Society, had no property and funds of its own. Shri Salwan started building the schools out of his own means when the land was allotted to the Trust. He had a flourishing contract business and other businesses from the profits or income of which he constructed school buildings. His initial effort was supplemented by a considerable grant in the neighbourhood of Rs 2 lakhs by the government for buildings and furniture. I am told that over Rs 5 lakhs have been spent on buildings and furniture and over three lakhs is the contribution of Shri Salwan from his own funds. In this situation, these institutions have always suffered from financial troubles. It stands to Shri Salwan's credit again that he not only brought into existence these institutions, but he also successfully ran them for a period of five years, from his own resources, supplemented as they were by government help. The latter, however, did not come regularly and payment of it was delayed on occasions.

In order to solve this problem, Shri Salwan started a number of concerns, namely a cinema, shops and a cafeteria. I, however, do not think that Shri Salwan has made any personal profit out of these concerns. His sole desire was to finance the schools with their income but that desire has been frustrated by events.

I am, however, convinced that the charges of embezzlement and misappropriation are not correct. A man who has spent so much from his own resources to build up the schools would not use for his own purpose any money belonging to the schools. As a matter of fact, the schools had no money to embezzle. All that possibly has happened is that, to tide over financial difficulties, funds given for one purpose have been used for another purpose, or loans have been taken for other school purposes from students' funds.

I do not find much substance in the allegations of maltreatment of members of the staff by Shri Salwan and the incidents to which my attention was drawn orally or in writing have been considerably exaggerated. It may well be that on occasion he was rude towards certain members of the staff, but at that time no capital was made of these incidents. These have been dug up after the trouble arose. No member of the staff actually maltreated has come to me with this complaint, except one female teacher, and on examining her I could not hold that she was in any manner treated roughly.

No subscriptions have been raised from the public for the Trust. I have not been able to see that the Trustees have contributed anything appreciable to the funds of the Society. Shri Salwan is the sole financier and builder of these schools.

Justice Hardy—A Snapshot

The extract and references printed herein are from Justice Hardyal Hardy's autobiography, *Struggles and Sorrows: The Personal Testimony of a Chief Justice* (published by Vikas Publication House in 1984):

A civil suit which created a great sensation was that filed by the Delhi administration under Section 92, Civil Procedure Code, against Girdhari Lal Salwan, a furniture maker, who had established a boys school, a girls school and a Montessori school in Rajendra Nagar, New Delhi. He was a carpenter from Kartarpur (Punjab) who had settled down in Peshawar in the NWFP. His own lack of education had created a great urge in him to see that his countrymen did not suffer for want of the same. He was a great artisan and was one of the foremost makers of modern furniture.

Justice Hardyal Hardy: former chief justice of the Delhi High Court.

The rehabilitation ministry had Mehr Chand Khanna as an advisor. Mehr Chand also came from Peshawar and knew what useful work G.L. Salwan had done in the educational field. He thus allotted a large slice of barren land in a hilly area where a refugee colony for housing Hindu refugees from Pakistan was going to be built.

G.L. Salwan spent thousands of rupees to develop the rocky soil and built the first high school known as the Salwan Higher Secondary School for Boys in that colony, which came to be known as Rajendra Nagar after Dr Rajendra Prasad, the first president of India. The boys school was followed by Salwan Higher Secondary School for Girls. A Montessori school was also established. Although the government gave him a few lakhs for building furniture, laboratories etc., Salwan himself contributed the major amount of money for setting up these institutions. The schools developed into splendid educational institutions. The government was proud of them. Foreign statesmen and dignitaries were invited to see these institutions as models of refugee enterprise in Delhi. Salwan created a trust to manage these schools.

I was responsible for preparing the memorandum and rules and regulations of the trust known as the Salwan Education Trust. Salwan did not agree with some of the rules and had his own way. I did not object to the changes he made.

These institutions had been built by him without taking any contributions from the public. The government's contribution towards the buildings was also meagre. The problem arose when some of the money given to the Trust by the government for a particular purpose was spent by Salwan on something else. The schools had not paid salaries to their teachers for several months, and this resulted in trouble between the teachers and Salwan.

The case came up for hearing before Gyan Chand Jain, subordinate judge first class—he is today a judge of Delhi High Court. He was, and is, a very learned and able judge. His knowledge of civil law is remarkably good. He is a man of great integrity, impartial and industrious. The government was represented by Inder Dev Dua, who later became a judge of the Punjab High Court. He was chief justice of Delhi High Court and then a judge of the Supreme Court of India. An erudite and learned scholar of law, he is thoroughly virtuous. His industry and impartiality are well-known. Jokingly I used to say that Justice Dua was the only man whom God created for integrity because this was how Justice Dua felt, implying that the rest of humanity lacked this quality. Arguments were heard at great length. Finally, Gyan Chand Jain rejected the government's application. The government pursued the matter to some extent but not with the previous determination.

Meanwhile, a police report was lodged by the superintendent of police, charging G.L. Salwan, Fakir Chand, the manager of the boys school, and two others. The committal proceedings went on before M.N.K. Yusefzai, additional district magistrate, Delhi.

The cross-examination in this case would have resulted in the accused being discharged which would have meant great saving of time and expense but Yusefzai, who heard elaborate arguments on behalf of the prosecution and the accused, committed the accused for trial. The government appointed Ram Lal Agarwal, additional sessions judge, Delhi as special judge and the case proceeded before him. I was assisted by Tilak Raj Bhasin, and his son Lalit Bhasin.

I remember well the occasion when Salwan came to my office accompanied by Bakshi Ghulam Mohammad, chief minister of Jammu and Kashmir. My fee was paid by Bakshi Sahib. Salwan had no money and Bakshi Sahib as his friend had given him Rs 50,000. I felt ashamed when I learnt this and refused to accept the amount. I was however told that the fee was a gift from a friend to a friend. Bakshi Sahib valued the educational work done by Salwan to help the refugees and treated the amount as a gift to a person who was short of funds to defend himself. I accepted the amount. When I mentioned the incident to Bhasin he too was greatly impressed.

Several interesting things happened in connection with the case against Salwan and his co-accused. Two interesting incidents are worth recording. Rajni Kumar was the principal of Salwan Higher Secondary School for Girls. She was one of the most important prosecution witnesses. She had a lot of complaints against Salwan's management of the school. Although the government had given grants for purchase of laboratory equipment for the school, Salwan had not made any purchases for the laboratory and had instead spent the money on payment of salaries to the teachers. Salwan was required to pay 5 per cent of the teachers' salaries from the Trust, the remaining 95 per cent came from the government. However he had spent the government money on construction of some rooms in the school and later, when the Trust had funds, he purchased the laboratory equipment. There were several other complaints. Salwan wanted me to ask her how he treated the female teachers. She said: 'Salwan treats every female teacher as his sister or daughter.' She admitted that it was at her insistence that the government grant for laboratory equipment was spent for payment of salaries to the teachers. Later Salwan bought the laboratory equipment with his own money.

The other interesting incident relates to another important witness. Sharma, who was the principal of Salwan Higher Secondary School for Boys, was to be examined the next day. Salwan had approached him through his friends to request him to speak the truth. His statement to the police was full of lies. Salwan somehow felt that the police would insist upon his sticking to the police statement. I believe a certain amount of pressure must have been put on him to speak the truth. In the morning the witness saw the special public prosecutor and came to court with him. He did not stick to his police statement and gave evidence in favour of the accused. The special public prosecutor thereupon made an application for cancellation of bail of the accused. I opposed the cancellation which was rejected.

The case proceeded and ultimately resulted in the conviction of Salwan and the accounts clerk. Fakir Chand was acquitted. I filed an appeal on behalf of Salwan. H.L. Anand filed an appeal on behalf of the accounts clerk. Justice G.D. Khosla, a judge of the Punjab High Court, admitted the appeals and released both the accused on bail. Ram Lal Agarwal had acquitted Salwan in respect to thirty charges and convicted him on charges which, according to me, could not be sustained. The appeal was heard in Delhi for a few days but since the term of the judges in the Circuit Bench at Delhi was about to expire it was transferred to Chandigarh.

Ram Lal Anand, who was a very competent lawyer, was appointed by the state to be its counsel. The hearing lasted eighteen days in Delhi and Chandigarh combined. Both the accused were acquitted. The acquittal of Salwan gave great impetus to him. However, the case and the anxiety faced by Salwan during its proceedings ruined his health.

The credit for the success of all the schools must necessarily go to Shiv Dutt Salwan. It is astonishing that in the days of his father, Girdhari Lal, the Trust had no funds. In the days of his son there is no dearth of money. The reason is simple. Shiv Dutt Salwan is a stickler for rules. He has mastered the Delhi Education Act, 1973, and the rules framed thereunder. He would not do anything nor would he allow anyone else to do anything unless the step is authorized by the Act.

I am glad to be associated with the Salwan Education Trust and its school and college. Education has always been dear to me, and if I had the money I would have built similar institutions for educating the children of my countrymen. Fortunately, the late Girdhari Lal and his son, Shiv Dutt Salwan, have afforded me the same opportunity. As chairman I am doing what I would have done if the institutions had been established by me. Shiv Dutt Salwan, whom I treat as my son, has given me complete control to run these institutions, for which I am grateful to him. May his prosperity increase.

The *Bull's Eye* was a newspaper which had initially brought a lot of negativity to the reputation of Girdhari Lal. But after the award, Anant Singh, the editor of *Bull's Eye*, issued an apology:

> I am since convinced that all the articles that appeared in the *Bull's Eye* against Shri G.L. Salwan were based on misrepresented facts supplied to us and their publication as such is very much regretted. It has now been brought to my notice that they were baseless.
>
> I am indeed sorry for the inconvenience and trouble caused to Shri G. L. Salwan. I am grateful to him for having agreed to drop the proceedings against me.

On 16 January 1961, Girdhari Lal Salwan was acquitted by the main branch of the Delhi High Court (at that time Delhi was under the legal jurisdiction of Punjab High Court). In spite of the award for the Salwan schools, as announced by Mehr Chand Mahajan, the media trial continued. This was the trial that would ruin his health.

TRIBUTE

Surinder Kaur Randhawa was the vice principal of Salwan Girls Senior Secondary School. Her husband Prof G.S. Randhawa, former vice chancellor of the Guru Nanak Dev University, Amritsar, pays his tribute to Pandit Salwan's personality. He says, 'In fact, I have hardly heard anything of Girdhari Lal's personal life which would do him any sort of discredit. He was very stern, though not rigid. He was a remarkable man in every way. He was like an uncut diamond. The school is the legacy of a tradition set up by Salwan. There is a couplet in Urdu:

Hazaron saal nargis apni benoori pe roti hai,
Barhi mushkil se hota hai chaman mein deedawar paida.

—Iqbal

For thousands of years narcissus bewails his sightlessness. It is after a long interval that a person with a vision is born.

'Let me sum him up with another couplet in Urdu,

Chala jaata hoon hasta khelta mauje havadis
Agar aasaniya hoti to zindagi dushwar ho jaye.

I go ahead enjoying, facing adversities and kicking up odd situations.
If adversities did not exist, life would be tasteless and meaningless for me.'

Through the Prism of Service Before Self

An Invocation

*I have had my invitation to this world's festival,
and thus my life has been blessed. My eyes have seen
and my ears have heard.*

*It was my part at this feast to play upon
my instrument, and I have done all I could.*

*Now, I ask, has the time come at last
when I may go in and see thy face and offer thee
my silent salutation?*

—Rabindranath Tagore
Gitanjali/Lyric 16

Girdhari Lal—the Politician

Girdhari Lal knew that for bringing about any major social revolution, he would have to ally himself with the government. Thus began his political journey.

Seeing life from close quarters made Girdhari Lal realize that his past work, honesty and straightforward approach to governance would prove to be his able allies. He decided to fight the Delhi state legislative assembly elections in 1952. Being associated with Congressman Mehr Chand Khanna made his path easier. He had the foresight to realize the limitations of being part of a dominant party like the Congress. He was fully aware of how and when a party's thinking could become a major obstacle in his mission. He decided to field himself as an independent candidate, supported by the Jana Sangh.

Trilochan Singh sums up the political scenario in those days. 'The year 1952 witnessed the first general elections of independent India. Sucheta Kriplani, I and several others resigned from the Congress as our demand for more seats for refugees fell on deaf ears. I headed the revolt and we all contested against the Congress. Sucheta Kriplani stood for the Lok Sabha seat from Paharganj constituency in New Delhi against the Congress and won. I was her chief election campaigner. I also happened to be the main speaker on the platform for Salwan, who was contesting as an independent candidate from Paharganj. He faced a formidable and a very rich opponent in Bawa Bachhitar Singh from the Congress. Apart from being rich and influential, Bawa Sahib used to brag, "Main toh chaandi ki jooti mar kar vote loonga" (I will win by the force of money power). People were aghast at this statement and expressed their disgust at the hustings. Bawa Bachhitar Singh lost the elections.'

History revealed that the election was an uneven contest. On the one hand there was the veteran, wealthy Bawa Bachhitar Singh, and on the other side was a refugee. If the former was the uncrowned king of Delhi, the latter was a commoner. One was supported by the strongest political umbrella, the Congress. The other was fired by the will to change the course of governance for thousands of refugees. In fact, it is recorded by one of Girdhari Lal's biographers that Bawa Bachhitar Singh was so overconfident and arrogant that he sarcastically advised Girdhari Lal stating: 'You are a Brahmin. You just look after your school and the daily prayers. Don't get into the murky and expensive business of politics and elections.' Not to be deterred from their mission, in stark contrast to the pomp and show of his opponent's campaign, Girdhari Lal and his supporters planned, delegated and worked quietly.

The commitment and strong belief in the leadership resulted in an extensive and extremely effective door-to-door campaign. Their work and efforts often got lost in the overt and boisterous Bawa Bachhitar Singh shows, but the Salwan camp carried on relentlessly. Sharan Kaur, daughter of Sardar Pyara Singh Saund, one of the prominent members of the team, often closes her eyes and recalls, 'I was very young at that time, but I remember how hard my father worked in those days, going door to door, house to house and not bothering to stop for food or personal life—all that took a back seat. When Pandit Salwan finally won everyone celebrated. Tears, smiles, hugs were seen across the faces of all.'

The door-to-door campaign did what lots of money and the

arrogance of power could not do. People knew Girdhari Lal and his grassroots work. This campaign actually brought people closer to the crusader in many ways. It was this unique emphasis on the worker as the beneficiary that won Girdhari Lal the election against all odds.

The resilience of Girdhari Lal's character was evident. He fought as an independent candidate from Paharganj and not from Rajendra Nagar. Bawa Bachhitar Singh lost by 258 votes. He filed an election petition but it was dismissed by Justice Gurudev Singh.

Girdhari Lal the legislator was truly the common man's person, easily accessible with his down-to-earth approach. He endeared himself so well to the constituents that he soon became a confidant for many of them. He spent a lot of time trying to understand the needs of the people, whether minor or major, and worked hard to deliver all that he had promised. Girdhari Lal could easily empathize with the masses as he was one of them and not 'removed and placed upon a pedestal' like many other politicians. He devoted extra efforts towards the housing issues, understanding very well that the remaining issues could be resolved once the need for a dwelling had been addressed. He became the torchbearer of development in Paharganj by constructing many two-storied buildings near the Amardas gurdwara for refugees.

For five years, Girdhari Lal worked with a deep sense of involvement driven by the positive reinforcement of seeing social fulfilment through a political platform. However, his political journey ended in 1957 with the dissolution of the Delhi assembly. The background to the dissolution was the ruling party's cupful of internal problems and multifarious differences amongst the key members within the Congress. The last straw was the cold war between Choudhary Brahm Prakash and Jag Pravesh Chandra. Hence, the Government of India dissolved the assembly and converted it into a metropolitan council. Disillusioned, Girdhari Lal never contested again and dedicated himself to enhancing the network of Salwan Schools in his mission of 'Education for All.'

Girdhari Lal—the Social Reformer

Apart from being an educationist, Girdhari Lal was also an active social reformer. He was against social dogmas and championed the cause of emancipation from disgraceful traditions like dowry. He set the perfect example by not giving and not accepting dowry. Added to these noble thoughts was the power of simplicity. Such was his obsession with simplicity that the functions for the weddings of his sons and daughters were attended by only fifteen people. Shiv Dutt recalls, 'Only fifteen people went from Peshawar Cantonment (for the wedding of Brahm Dutt) to Sultanpur Lodhi, in the Kapurthala district. There was no electricity; we stayed in the temple lodge. The marriage was a simple affair without dowry.' Kaushaliya was the girl in question. She only had one brother and no father. The marriage was solemnized in the morning and in the evening the barat returned.

Raj Kumari, who married Shiv Dutt, was from Banga district, Jalandhar. She had no father. Her brother, who was in the army, wanted to go to Delhi to perform the wedding as the town did not have any electricity. But Girdhari Lal was firm and said that weddings are for uniting the hearts and binding the families and not for ostentatious displays. Urmila, from

Kapurthala district, Punjab, married Ramesh Dutt. Ten people went to Kapurthala and performed the wedding. Girdhari Lal wanted good daughters-in-law. There were no other expectations of any kind.

The daughters' weddings were also very simple. Santosh Rani's husband was in the Indian Army. In those days, the marriage party usually stayed at the girl's place for two to three days. But Girdhari Lal refused to participate in this tradition. From Jalalabad, Punjab, the marriage party went to Peshawar. They only stayed for one night and returned. Ved Rani's marriage was fixed at Kapurthala, Punjab. The boy was in the government service. The boy's family and close relatives wanted to see the 15 August celebrations in Delhi (as the marriage was on 13 August). Girdhari Lal refused to pay for their expenses.

He was in favour of the re-marriage of widows. When Brahm Dutt died, Girdhari Lal wanted Kaushaliya to get married again. But she refused. She said that she was married to the family and the future of her two children was only in this family.

Besides being opposed to the scourge of dowry, Girdhari Lal rehabilitated many women who were widowed during the Peshawar riots by getting them remarried. He was also against any kind of discrimination based on class or caste. To promote this spirit of equality, he appointed a Harijan as a waterman in the school so that the spirit of equality and fellow feeling be inculcated in the students.

An aide of a prominent leader of Jammu and Kashmir was arrested and placed in the Central Jail in Jammu. He was married but he had relations with a Hindu lady working in the jail and had a child by her. He told her to convert to Islam and said he would accept her as his wife. She refused his offer, but was forced to convert. The Hindus in Jammu agitated and went on strike. Another prominent leader requested Girdhari Lal to receive the Hindu lady in Delhi in order to quell the agitation. She came to 37, Pusa Road, New Delhi with the child. Girdhari Lal advised her to re-marry. Dev Prakash Shastri, a teacher who had lost his first wife, was willing to marry her. The Hindu lady was purified through Arya Samaj rites. Girdhari Lal did the 'kanyadaan' and provided them accommodation.

During the 1962 war between India and China, Girdhari Lal collected Rs 35,000 and donated it to the government. His family also donated their jewellery and cash.

Girdhari Lal—the Environmentalist

The morning hours have a natural association with freshness, beauty and creativity, as if the entire spectrum is energized by a unique catalyst. Girdhari Lal was himself the morning catalyst in the school, heralding a beautiful beginning to every day. Come rain or shine, he was on the school campus by 7 a.m. He would first visit the grounds in his daily round of the school.

The gardeners and other workers listened very attentively to him. The campus was full of beautiful flowers. There were roses in all hues with chrysanthemums of all shapes and colours giving the campus a bright and inviting touch. Girdhari Lal would interact with the gardeners every day and knew everything about the planting schedules of different saplings. He was an expert at differentiating the winter and summer flowers, and insisted that no one should pluck flowers from the school campus. He knew all the leaves of the trees and plants in the premises. He knew how many lemons there were on each lemon tree, and would start enquiring even if one lemon was found missing.

Shiv Dutt remembers how his father chided a young teacher who picked a red rose to adorn her hair. He told her, 'Beta, baat suno, yeh rose vahan laga hua tha . . . bura lagta tha tumhe? Tumne baal pe lagaya . . . baalon ke ander toh sookh jayega . . . toh tum phenk doge . . . Kya vahan paudhe pe pada hua burra lagta tha…saari duniya dekhti usko.' (My daughter, was the rose not looking nice on the rose bush? You have pinned it in your hair; it will soon wither and you will throw it. Was it not looking nice on the sapling where it would have been admired by all?).

Deshbandhu Chawla, one of the students of Amar Vidyalaya who joined Salwan Boys School, has vivid memories of the early days of the school: 'It was a great experience shifting from the hutments of Amar Vidyalaya to a neatly constructed Salwan Boys School. Shri D.N. Datta was the principal. I remember Pandit G.L. Salwan as a strict disciplinarian who was concerned about greenery and the environment. As the school campus was coming up, all the students were brought to the ground during P.T. periods and were asked to pick up small stones and pebbles from the ground to make it neat and clean. The students were motivated to perform this task, as those who picked up the maximum pebbles were given a reward, as well as a pat on the back by Pandit G.L. Salwan.'

His love for nature is portrayed through an anecdote linked to his health. When he was taken ill, Girdhari Lal visited the Christian Medical College, Vellore. Upon arrival, he noticed very tall Ashoka trees. He was fascinated by their strong trunks and green foliage. He realized that the south Indian variety of the trees was different from the trees in Delhi. He wanted similar Ashoka trees in the Salwan school campus too. As per his instructions, 200 saplings were bought and transported by train from Vellore to Delhi.

On returning to Delhi, though still not in the best of health, he was highly elated when informed that the 200 Ashoka saplings had found a new home on the campus. It was a visual feast where every flower, sapling and tree was just the way nature intended it to be, with sparkling water nurturing its growth. For Girdhari Lal, nature always revived hope, overcoming despair.

Girdhari Lal and the Religion of Humanity

The greatest religion for him was the 'religion of humanity' and he believed that true religion leads a man to wisdom. Girdhari Lal provided financial assistance to poor students, ensuring that they had a nutritious diet for mental alertness and sound health.

He said that education should not only aim at mental development but also at developing the physical and moral faculties. He laid great stress on the religious education of the students. For him, discipline was the soul of any institution or organization.

Although he did not visit temples but he was a devout devotee of Lord Krishna. There was no differentiation between the Sanatan Dharam and Arya Samaj practices. He was liberal and progressive in thought and believed that religion is personal. The house in Kartarpur where the Salwan family

श्री ब्राह्मण सभा (रजि०), राजेन्द्र नगर, नई देहली
कार्य-कारिणी सभा
नवम्बर १९६२

G.L. Salwan with members of the Brahman Samaj in 1962.

stayed before Partition has been, since then, donated to the Arya Samaj temple.

He read the Bhagwad Gita's eighteenth chapter regularly: 'Be intent on the action, not on the fruits of action. Any action performed in a selfless spirit is superior.'

He offered flowers to God every morning. If any needy person met him on auspicious religious occasions, like Sankranti, he gave him money. He fed the birds every morning, before eating his breakfast.

Girdhari Lal helped people but did not boast about it to his family or ever ask for his money back. Bodhraj, a refugee from Peshawar settled in Kanpur, met Shiv Dutt two months after

Girdhari Lal's death. According to him, he had borrowed Rs 20,000 in 1955 to establish his business. Shiv Dutt refused at first to accept the money but Bodhraj insisted, saying that his conscience would prick him. So Shiv Dutt accepted it and deposited it with the Trust.

Salwan Boys Senior Secondary School and Salwan Girls Senior Secondary School impart free education to students, most of whom are from the less privileged groups. There are more than 2500 students in these two schools. The Trust gives them money from its own resources, including grants and scholarships up to postgraduate level. The vision of the founder, who wanted every child, irrespective of his or her financial, social or religious background, to get the best possible education is being fulfilled in the process.

Yash Oberoi adds: 'When I completed my class X studies, my father asked Shri G.L. Salwan to help me get some work. He suggested that I make a shop in the small area under the stairs of the school building. The shop exists even today.'

Not only to Yash but to other refugees as well, Girdhari Lal rented out shops carved out from the school building to rehabilitate them. He offered them these premises at a very low rent.

Role of Women in the Family

Parvati Devi, Girdhari Lal's sister, became a widow at an early age. She devoted the rest of her life to promoting the cause her brother was so dearly committed to.

Girdhari Lal's wife, Gyan Devi, daughter of Ratanchand from Mukerian, Punjab, was deeply rooted in Indian traditions. Gyan Devi studied till middle school. She worked with a

Parvati Devi dedicated her life to supporting her brother Girdhari Lal Salwan's cause of social development, particularly women's welfare.

missionary zeal to propagate the virtues of Indian culture and simplicity.

Raj Salwan, the daughter-in-law of Girdhari Lal, has sacrificed everything, all the luxuries, desires and material gains, to impart the lesson that a good human being is greater than all other worldly gains. She came to the school only when invited, says Gayatri Sahai:

> She was a graceful lady, very humble and affectionate. The family members of Shri Salwan kept a low profile. Raj Salwan used to say, 'You teachers lay the real foundations of the school.' When the foundation stone ceremony of the library block was held, the teachers were called to do the honours.

Girdhari Lal's wife, Gyan Devi, welcomes Pandit Fakir Chand to Salwan School.

Raj Salwan, Girdhari Lal Salwan's daughter-in-law, welcomes Mother Teresa.

President Zakir Hussain with the members of the Salwan family.

The Circle of Life

Girdhari Lal Salwan had nurtured a large section of society that was still reeling from the pangs of the Partition. In spite of all efforts to rehabilitate the refugees, he was falsely implicated in cases that stood on frivolous technical grounds. The tension and negative media publicity took its toll on his health.

Before long, he fell ill and was admitted to the All India Institute of Medical Sciences in New Delhi for two months.

Trilochan Singh recalls an incident just before Girdhari Lal passed away on 22 October 1964, 'Girdhari Lalji had the first inkling of age when he fell ill and was advised to visit AIIMS in New Delhi. When he was admitted in a private ward at AIIMS, I used to be a regular visitor. He was in bad shape. His ailment had drained him. One day there was some flutter. A couple of rooms away, an old revolutionary from Punjab, Kedarnath Saigal, who had suffered a lot during the freedom movement, including life imprisonment, was admitted. I came to know that Jawaharlal Nehru was coming to see him. I told Salwan Sahib. I felt a bit of regret building inside him. I went to Kedarnath's room. When Panditji came I mustered courage and told him that there was another ailing freedom fighter in the next room—Salwan from Peshawar. He did not say anything, but quietly walked into Salwan's room. Panditji sat near him, patted him and wished him well and left. Girdhari Lal Salwan pressed my hands and I could feel that he felt good that the prime minister had visited him.'

Since a proper diagnosis of his ailment could not be determined, his dear friend Bakshi Ghulam Mohammad, with the wholehearted support and concern of the Government of India, referred him to an American doctor who was attending a conference in India. Raj Kumari Amrit Kaur, who was then the health minister of India, aided in this referral. The doctor attributed the cause of his failing health to his mental tension and depression and said that it would take some time to overcome. The Government of India wanted to send him to the US to recover, but Girdhari Lal refused.

Bakshi Ghulam Mohammad did not want his friend to just ebb away, so he took him along with his family to 'Chashma Shahi Huts' at the state government's expense. A renowned doctor, Dr Ali Jan, who was the chief neurologist of Maharaja Hari Singh Medical College, rendered proper diagnosis and treatment. After all the medical tests were concluded, Girdhari Lal was advised to go to Christian Medical College in Vellore.

Dr Chandi, the neuro head and director of Vellore Christian

Medical College, tried his best, but it was all in vain. He suggested that since the curative power of medicine was limited, perhaps time and nature alone should be solicited to heal the healer. Girdhari Lal's health continued to deteriorate and he breathed his last on 22 October 1964.

P.S. Chauhan (principal of Salwan Boys Senior Secondary School) and Salig Ram, a teacher from the same school, were with him till the last moments of his life. More than one lakh people were part of the procession which went to the ground for the last rites. On reaching the cremation ground at Panchkuian Road, there was a difference of opinion amongst the religious leaders on the rituals to be performed at the time of cremation. Ultimately, Girdhari Lal was cremated according to the Vedic rites. The Sikhs, followers of Sanatan Dharam, Arya Samajis and all political parties paid their tributes.

When Panditji died, his sister Parvati Devi murmured at his pyre, 'Brother, wait for a week. I will join you soon.' A week later, on 29 October 1964, she got up early in the morning and went to lie down on the same spot where her brother's body had been kept a week ago and murmured, 'Brother, here I come!' Her death came as an unbearable shock for the family, sending them into deep mourning.

Girdhari Lal's Alsatian dog, Teggi, also refused to move from his master's bedside for two weeks and gave up eating. A week after Parvati's demise, Teggi too breathed his last. Such was the bond between Girdhari Lal and his pet!

The municipal corporation passed a unanimous resolution and renamed the road (wherein the schools are situated) between Pusa Road and Shankar Road as Girdhari Lal Salwan Marg.

William Wordsworth's poem, 'Intimations of Immortality from Recollections of Early Childhood,' beautifully sums up Girdhari Lal Salwan:

There was a time when meadow, grove and stream,
The earth and every common sight,
To me did seem
Apparell'd in celestial light

The rainbow comes and goes,
And lovely is the rose;
The moon doth with delight,
Look round her when the heavens are bare;
Waters on a starry night
Are beautiful and fair;
The sunshine is a glorious birth;
But yet I know, where 'er I go,
That there pass'd away a glory from the earth.

The Temples of Wisdom: Leveraging a Legacy

An Invocation

Where the mind is without fear and the head is held high;
Where knowledge is free;

Where the world has not been broken up into fragments
by narrow domestic walls;

Where words come out from the depth of truth;

Where tireless striving stretches its arms
towards perfection;

Where the clear stream of reason has not lost its way
into the dreary desert sand of dead habit;

Where the mind is led forward by thee into ever-widening
thought and action—

Into that heaven of freedom, my Father,
let my country awake.

—Rabindranath Tagore
Gitanjali/Lyric 35

Introduction

Girdhari Lal opened a whole new world in and around Delhi, which continues to guide even the present-day generation. He did not let anyone take precedence over his mission. He knew a relationship works best when both individuals are balanced and do not become an obstacle in each other's lives. Assertiveness adds power and conviction to a message and enables a leader's voice to be heard. Assertive leaders also tend to communicate more often, as their passion leads them to capitalize on every opportunity they can find to deliver a message. Girdhari Lal was surely an assertive leader and that is why he left a great legacy. The Salwan Education Trust runs and manages eleven schools spread over the National Capital Region and a welfare centre in J.J. Slum Colony at Inderpuri. The Trust has twenty-four staff flats in Rajendra Nagar for the accommodation of the teaching and non-teaching staff of the schools. Committed to intellectual growth, the Salwan Schools have put in about seventy years of dedicated work.

Mission Education

> In my soul there is a temple, a shrine, a mosque, a church where I kneel. Prayer should bring us to an altar where no walls or names exist. Is there not a region of love where the sovereignty is illumined nothing, where ecstasy gets poured into itself and becomes lost, where the wing is fully alive but has no mind or body.
>
> —*Rabia al-Adawiyya al-Qaysiyya, 8th century C.E.*

The Salwan Education Trust surged ahead to establish unprecedented landmarks in the field of education, its momentum driven by the values, philosophy and vision inculcated by the passion of Girdhari Lal, to create educational foundations with a positive impact on society.

The mission continued from 1949 in independent India with the establishment of Salwan Boys Senior Secondary School at Rajendra Nagar. The first phase of schools in Rajendra Nagar was completed with the establishment of Salwan Public School (Afternoon) in 1991, which became and still remains an unrivalled education hub of the NCR, catering to different needs and economic strata of society and backed by the common values, philosophies and vision under the larger umbrella of the Salwan Foundation. The second phase saw the emergence of the first satellite unit outside the Rajendra Nagar campus with the opening of the Salwan Junior Public School at Naraina in 1993 and the Salwan Public School, Tronica City, Ghaziabad in 2005.

The schools established by the Trust, till now, are:

Salwan Boys Senior Secondary School	1949
Salwan Girls Senior Secondary School	1950
Salwan Montessori School, Rajendra Nagar	1952
Salwan Public School, Rajendra Nagar	1953
Salwan Social Welfare Centre	1970
G.D. Salwan College, Delhi University	1970-89
G.D. Salwan Public School	1990
Salwan Public School (Afternoon), Rajendra Nagar	1991
Salwan Junior Public School, Naraina	1993
Salwan Public School, Mayur Vihar, Phase III	1996
Salwan Public School, Sec-15, Gurgaon	1996
Salwan Montessori School, Sec-5, Gurgaon	1999
Salwan Public School, Tronica City, U.P.	2005

The expansion in eastern India was made possible in 1992 when the Trust was offered land, free of cost, by the Government of Sikkim, to open a school on 27 acres. The Trust felt it was a little too early to spread its wings in far-off areas. The trustees, all working with passion, without any monetary benefit, needed to consolidate the institutions in central India and hence, they deferred the plans to venture into Sikkim. Michelangelo has very appropriately said, 'Most people spend more time focusing on their weaknesses than developing their strengths. As a result of this, most people never connect with the greatness that it is their duty to discover.'

The Education Hub

Let us walk down memory lane to witness how these schools were created and what the main activities and achievements of these landmarks were. The philosophy of the Trust is not only to impart teaching but to develop the right attitudes, without which an individual can neither actualize his true potential nor contribute meaningfully to society. The vision is also to remove unnatural boundaries for a child, enabling the mind to be free, so that the flow of ideas is not restrained. Therefore, all the schools run by the Trust are aesthetically designed, keeping the concept of space in mind. A healthy and friendly environment synchronizes with the learning process. The institutions run under the aegis of the Trust draw inspiration from Tagore's words, hence all kinds of suppression are eliminated, as they firmly believe that creativity is stifled by fear.

The Trust believes in chasing dreams and is committed to providing freedom and space to each child to grow at his own pace. Its vision is to churn out thinkers, creators and leaders in every field. Firmly rooted in Indian culture, the constant endeavour of the Trust is to prepare Salwanians to accept the challenges of a global village, through promotion of inter-faith culture, tolerance and value-based education.

Salwan Boys Senior Secondary School

The Body and Soul of Brick and Mortar

Girdhari Lal would supervise the construction of school buildings and was led by the strong belief that the classrooms should have natural light, adequate ventilation and so forth as part of an environment conducive to the learning process. He believed in his people.

The Salwan Education Trust ensures that new blocks and classrooms are added periodically to replace the old

Salwan Boys Senior Secondary School, Rajendra Nagar.

infrastructure in order to enhance capacity in line with the growth projections. During the process of renovating the school building in Delhi, the transition of Salwan Boys School to its modern form with the legacy and the tradition of dedication and reverence still forms the basis of all actions for generations to come.

Such finer points have been brought out from the archives by Inder Dutt, an architect, who till today is in awe of Girdhari Lal's architectural skills. He says, 'I am convinced that my grandfather was influenced by Mughal architecture. The concept of nurturing big lawns and lots of flower beds was to provide a cooling effect to the hot winds blowing across. The usage of columns with grand pedestals further highlights the influence of a mind oriented towards grandeur. What amazes me the most is the positioning of the principal's office. The principals just had to step out of the office and by turning their neck a few degrees, the entire school campus with students and teachers came in focus. The round towers, an element of design so vividly used, were meant to be the music rooms, so that the classrooms would not be disturbed.'

In today's context, running an effective aided school and providing education at par with a good private unaided recognized school is extremely difficult due to the lack of autonomy. However, with utmost transparency and effective management, the aided schools run by the Trust have established a cordial relation with and very good reputation in the eyes of the Department of Education of Delhi, which extends all necessary help whenever required. Though a substantial amount is received from the Delhi government towards the salary of staff, the Trust is spending almost

35 per cent of the budgeted amount on the schools, which itself is a colossal amount.

The Salwan Boys Higher Secondary School, an aided private recognized school, has its objectives clear: to provide for all-round growth, character building, academic excellence and development of a global perspective in students. Living up to these expectations, the school has been recognized for sports and extracurricular activities. The earlier batches have produced officers for the Indian Administrative Service, the armed forces, as well as outstanding sportsmen, actors, lecturers and political leaders.

Now, as a matter of tradition, every year the students visit the Base Hospital of the Delhi cantonment to pay their respects to the custodians of our borders. On the basis of excellent overall grooming, students are absorbed by leading public sector undertakings and corporate houses. Regular participation in the annual Republic Day Parade celebrations is a unique feature of this aided school.

Sports being the school's forte, about forty students (on an average) play cricket at the national level. A select few participate, at the international level, in the junior and senior categories. The school has bagged the national and state championships in cricket in the last twenty years. The students have done extraordinarily well in cricket at the international level and won the championship in the 'World School Cricket' tournament.

The school has contributed many Test cricketers to the Indian team, including Vinay Lamba, Suresh Luthra, the late Raman Lamba, Ashish Nehra, Aakash Chopra, Amit Mishra, Pradeep Chawla and Rakesh Raman Jha.

Bakshi Ghulam Mohammad with Shiv Dutt Salwan and J.R. Mullick.

Students of the Salwan Boys School at the Republic Day Parade.

119

Participating players of the G.L. Salwan Hot Weather Cricket Tournament being introduced to Raj Salwan (extreme right).

The winning team from Salwan Boys School. The school won the Parle All India School Cricket Trophy for five consecutive years, a national record.

R. S. Dabas, former principal, was awarded the 'Best Teacher State Award' by Sheila Dikshit, chief minister of Delhi, on the occasion of Teachers' Day. Dabas, though a national-level volleyball player, had put his heart and soul into rejuvenating cricket in the school. With complete freedom given by the management, he created a passion for this game in his students.

The principals and academicians who have headed this school over the years are:

Principals	Year
D.N. Datta	1949–1955
P. D. Bhatia	1955–1959
P.S. Chauhan	1959–1966

From left to right: P.S. Chauhan (principal of Salwan Boys), Shiv Dutt Salwan and A.N. Jha (lieutenant governor of Delhi).

S.D. Sharma	1967–1976
S.N. Malik	1977–1981
B.L. Sharma	1981–1990
G.S. Sharma	1992–1998
I. D. Chandok	1998–2001
R.S. Dabas	2001–2008
Sharmistha Gupta	2009 –2011
Saroj Achre	2011 to present

Salwan Girls Senior Secondary School

The second flagship school, established by Girdhari Lal during his lifetime, is the Salwan Girls School. It is a great institution of its kind, giving an opportunity to thousands of girls to educate themselves and face the world on their own terms. This institution was established immediately after Partition, and was a great source of inspiration to young girls. Rajni Kumar, the founder-principal, took it upon herself to give the institution the vision of the founder.

The school, in the heart of Delhi, provides opportunities to girls in many ways, besides encouraging them to join the armed forces. The challenges this institution faces are huge given the background of the students, but the school has never created any distinction amongst the students for any reason or in any manner. The school has churned out brilliant students. Janak Juneja (IAS), a former student of this school and now a Trustee of Salwan Education Trust, cherishes her time here. Her faith in Salwan's schools made her take a conscious decision to give a scholarship to the meritorious students on a regular basis.

In the mid 1990s, the management felt the need for a change

Salwan Girls Senior Secondary School: Empowering the girl child.

from the mindset prevalent in the neighbourhood—that the girl child did not want to study and was content washing clothes, cooking and cleaning the floor. These attitudes were firmly entrenched and posed a considerable challenge since this school was also catering to the economically weak children.

The girls who participated in various sports were served milk, sprouts, nimbu-paani and other nutritious foods prepared in the home science lab to enhance their strength and stamina. This endeavour boosted and encouraged more girls to participate, as most of them were coming to school on empty stomachs. Gur-chana was given to provide adequate protein and iron to the weak and anaemic girls.

Specialists from Rajputana Rifles, with whom the school had a warm relationship, along with members within the school ranks, formed the core team whose responsibility was to inject life into this school. Salwan Girls School excels at the zonal level, the inter-zonal level and has won laurels at the state and national level in sports. High altitude training at Nehru Institute for Mountaineering, Uttarkashi, and the Himalayan Mountaineering Institute at Darjeeling has been a great success in this school. The students are also exposed to the regimental centres of the Infantry Directorate of the Indian Army located at Subatu, Ooty, Lansdowne, Pachmarhi and other centres. Salwan Girls School has bagged a number of medals at national and international events and been adjudged the 'Best School' in Delhi for sports for three consecutive years.

Home Science became one of the mainstays of the school, providing girls with the requisite platform to hone their natural skills in art and craft, home management as well as giving them practice in how to plan, prepare and provide nutritious and healthy food to their families. The making of a good home is a talent which the coming generation tends to forget, but in this school, the values are so deeply imbedded that every student is sure of giving her family a happy and secure home. Another beautiful part of this institution is that many students, after excelling in higher education, join the school as teachers to return to the society what they gained from it, a true service to the community.

The school's well-equipped, independent, eco-friendly computer lab, science labs and music rooms, sports and NCC cover all aspects of modern education. The school's participation in the closing ceremony of the Commonwealth Games 2010 was a great experience for the students. Besides this, the students regularly participate in the annual Republic

Sardar Swaran Singh (former defence minister) decorating an NCC cadet from Salwan Girls School. Also seen in the picture are P.C. Chaudhry (extreme left) and Ramesh Dutt Salwan (centre).

Day parade. Vijay Mala Bhanot, an international athlete, and a former student, was conferred the Arjuna Award in 1994. There are many such students whose achievements, if listed, would cover more than a few pages. Among other recent honours, the students of Class X and XII were awarded the 'Indira Award 2011'; and the school was honoured with the Alankaran Award with a cash prize of Rs 50,000 from the Delhi administration in 2006. Among the teachers, Surinder Randhawa, PGT (history) was given the state award in 1983; Prem Lata Nijhawan, PGT (vocal music) was conferred the state award in 2003 and Alka Sibbal, PGT (home science) was conferred the state award in 2005.

*Y.B. Chavan (Union defence minister) visits the school, accompanied by
J.R. Mullick (left) and Shiv Dutt Salwan (right).*

Vice President G.S. Pathak visits the school accompanied by
M.R. Kohli (extreme left), Shiv Dutt Salwan (centre) and J.R. Mullick (right).

Over the years, the school has been led by the following principals:

Principals	*Year*
Rajni Kumar	1950–1955
V. Sood	1956–1960
Raj Suri	1960–1964
S. Sachdeva	1964–1989
V. Rajeshwari	1989–1999
R. Kohli	1999–2003
Adarsh Sharma	2003–2010
Indu Bala	2010 to present

The Salwan Marathon

The fact that Girdhari Lal considered physical fitness an essential pre-requisite to good education cannot be over-emphasized. Added to this is the larger social context in which he viewed the real 'application' of the acquired education. Under his leadership, many initiatives were taken towards the fulfilment of this 'holistic' objective, providing a very strong sense of direction to the overall strategy. In recent times the most significant idea that is positioned in line with this objective is the 'Salwan Marathon', which forms a fitting tribute to the vision of the founder.

The marathon made a humble beginning as a 'race'. The race was a sequel to the sports activities initiated to bring out

Salwan Marathon: Strengthening mind, body and soul.

the spirit of courage and determination in the children. In 1995, the success of Salwan Girls School students at the inter-zonal level led to the conception of a race with 300 students, called the 'Salwan Marathon'. Started with a budget of just Rs 2500, the race proved to be a great success among the students of Delhi. From that humble beginning, the Salwan Marathon now attracts over 47,000 participants from all over India and abroad. This undoubtedly is due to the untiring efforts of Inder Dutt and the team, which made every part of it possible.

Successive editions of the Salwan Marathon have been held at the Jawaharlal Nehru Stadium and later shifted to the picturesque location of the Nicholson Range, Brar square, Delhi cantonment. As a product of the 'Mission Sports' initiative, the Salwan Marathon provides an opportunity to reinforce the basic values of joy of effort, fair play, respect for others, pursuit of excellence and balance between the mind, body and will. The Salwan Marathon is now synonymous with sports for children and is viewed by over 10 million people from all over India and abroad. This has come to be acknowledged as the largest road race in the country and recognized by the Athletic Federation of India. It is now conducted with the help of the Air Force Sports Control Board, the Rajputana Rifles and the Delhi Athletic Association.

The various sports initiatives establish that 'sports can achieve results beyond sports', reinforcing Girdhari Lal's philosophy.

Salwan Montessori School, Rajendra Nagar

Salwan Montessori School is where the foundation of every child is laid, with a blend of the Montessori and Reggio Emilia

Salwan Montessori School, Rajendra Nagar, New Delhi.

Children of Salwan Montessori participating in a cultural show.

systems and demonstrates the 'true cause of education'. From a humble beginning, the school has risen to great heights. In the field of pre-school education, it occupies a place of eminence today.

Learning is the way of life at Salwan Montessori School, which is the result of planning, teamwork and commitment to excellence. The school provides superlative indoor and outdoor facilities and organizes content-rich activities involving children, parents and society, spreading messages of peace and humanity. At the age of three to five years, children are trained in the fields of sports and culture and are given ample opportunities to showcase their learning instincts and talents. Besides the traditional 3 R's of reading, writing and arithmetic, the school develops the 3 R's of respect, responsibility and relationships.

Embedded in the system is the emphasis on physical development through training programmes conducted by professionals. The activities at Salwan Montessori School adopt a rounded approach with diverse tools to make the child a complete individual. Encouraging joint family ties and bonding with grandparents, inculcating the habit of service to the nation through blood donation camps organized by the parents for the last eighteen years, and sharing community festivals and food is what the school is respected for in the NCR.

On his visit to the school in 2008, Dr A.P.J. Abdul Kalam, former president of India, appreciated the efforts of the Trust in the following words: 'Sixty years of growth of the Salwan group of schools is indeed impressive. For the past six decades, the Salwan Schools have generated many leaders in different fields. My best wishes to all the members of the Salwan

*Dr A.P.J. Abdul Kalam, former president of India (centre) at an event to honour the
students of the school. From left to right: Maj Gen J.K. Kapoor, Shiv Dutt Salwan,
Sabeer Bhatia, Justice Jaspal Singh and Sardar Harpal Singh.*

educational community for success in their mission of
providing value based education to the youth of Delhi and
NCR.'

Ramesh Bijlani, who has had a distinguished career,
remembers his first school, Salwan Montessori, in 1953.

'My father chose to send me to SMS although most children
from the neighbourhood went to a government school, and
even he could ill-afford the fees that education at SMS required.
My father could send me to SMS because SMS existed, and
SMS existed because of Shri G.L. Salwan. In that sense, Shri
Salwan was the other instrument of God that shaped my life. I
am happy, and honoured, to pay this humble tribute to Shri
Salwan on the occasion of the Founder's Day.'

The inspiring individuals who shaped the Montessori into a
sought-after school, are:

Principals	Year
Indu Kapur	1965–1980
P .Verma	1980–1992
George Kunnekel	1992–1994
P. Joglekar	1994–2007
Anuradha Mathur	2007 to present

Salwan Public School, Rajendra Nagar

The school is known for its unparalleled academic record. In 1974, a number of students from Salwan Public School ranked among the best at the all-India level. The same year the 6th, 7th and 10th rank in the humanities stream of the Central Board of Secondary Education (CBSE) were bagged by the

Salwan Public School, Rajendra Nagar, New Delhi.

students of the school. The following year, the school notched up the 2nd, 3rd, 4th, 5th, 6th, 7th and 9th ranks in the Board exams. In 1976, the school excelled with top ranks in the CBSE in the science and commerce group. All 113 students who took the XI Board exam got first divisions, thereby creating a record. The first rank holder in CBSE science group batch of 1976 was Ashish Nanda, the son of one of the teachers of the school. He went on to top IIT Delhi and IIM Ahmedabad and is presently a professor at the Harvard Business School. The school has continued to maintain an excellent record both in academics and sports. In the session 2005-06, twelve students from Class XII were awarded merit certificates by the CBSE.

N. Sharma joined as a teacher in 1966 and retired in February 2003 as the vice principal of the school. He says: 'It is because of the good students and hard working teachers that we excelled in academics. I remember all the teachers putting in sincere effort and the management also encouraged us. It was a very good academic atmosphere.'

Today, the Inclusive School Programme initiated by the school caters to the needs of the differently abled students as well as those afflicted by learning disorders. The school is home to many visually impaired children who study in a happy, vibrant and sensitive environment conducive to the growth of their self-confidence and self-reliance This inclusive education is not only unique but a great experience for others, as it creates bonding and great peer relations.

The school provides freedom and space to each child to grow at his/her pace and reach his/her optimum potential through a number of activities. Under the aegis of the 'Future Cities

India 2020' programme, the Salwan Public School bagged the first prize for the Best Computer Model on the topic 'Re-development of Chandni Chowk'. The school takes pride in being a pioneer in environment-related issues. Nearly two kilometres of the Ridge road was adopted by the school and more than 2,000 saplings planted in the Ridge area as part of the Go Green Campaign.

The school has left its mark on the prestigious Republic Day Parade at Rajpath, being adjudged the best in cultural items in 1986 and 1988 and getting second position in 1987. The school has also had the courage to bet on the dreams of its students and faculty members. Staging *Mirza Ghalib*, *Heer Ranjha*, *50 years of Bollywood Music* and *The Great Music Directors* are some of the many challenges accepted by the students, and their fantastic performances impressed the viewers. The former chief justice of India, Justice R.C. Lahoti as well as Tom Alter, Muzaffar Ali and the members of the Ghalib Institute were spellbound by the spectacular performance of the students, who did a live show on the life of Mirza Ghalib. Anand Raj Anand, a former student of the sister institution, Salwan Boys School, was mesmerized when he watched the excellent performance of the students and he said, 'After watching the students, I am sure that Bollywood will never have a dearth of talent.'

The 'G.L. Salwan Hot Weather Cricket Tournament' is organized by the school in memory of its founder. Most of the Indian team players consider it a matter of prestige to participate in this tournament and surely, for many, it functioned as a prelude to their entry into the national team.

General P.P. Kumaramangalam giving away a trophy at a school event.

P.C. Chaudhry, principal of Salwan School, being conferred the Padma Shri by President V.V. Giri in 1976.

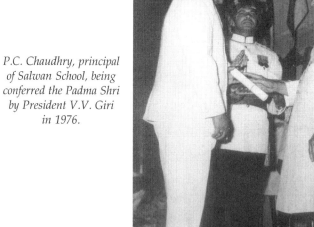

Mr Bhatt, director of Department of Education, with P.C. Chauhan, Shiv Dutt Salwan, S. Sachdeva and P.C. Chaudhry.

President S. Radhakrishnan with Shiv Dutt Salwan at a school function.

Babu Jagjivan Ram, Union labour minister, with Shiv Dutt Salwan.

Babu Jagjivan Ram with the faculty of the Salwan Schools.

Lal Bahadur Shastri with S.D. Salwan and family and principals of the Salwan Schools.

Prime Minister Manmohan Singh was presented a cheque of Rs 16 lakhs towards the PM's Relief Fund for tsunami victims in 2005, on behalf of the Salwan Education Trust.

His Holiness the Dalai Lama with faculty members of the Salwan Schools in 1998.

Staying connected, even during periods of peace, with the jawans and officers of the armed and paramilitary forces is a token of affection from the Salwanians. Since the Kargil War (2000), the school has hosted a 'Mahabhoj' for the jawans, officers and widows of the martyrs. While employing staff, the Trust gives preference to them. Many army generals and other very senior officers have saluted the students for the affection showered on the jawans and officers and have all sworn that they have never seen such respect from any organization in this country. Tears have rolled and smiles have shone on these momentous occasions.

The Ramesh Dutt block, the 'Brahm Vatika' and the L.D. Gupta block are named after the trustees and senior officers of the school who served the institutions with passion and selfless interest. Every new additions made in the school are inaugurated by the toppers, leaving his/her mark on the school building forever.

The strong pillars behind this success who led the school as principals are:

Principals	*Year*
G.C. Sharma	1953–1967
P.C. Chaudhry	1967–1977
Kuldeep Rai	1977–1980
S.N. Malik	1980–1980
O.L. Henderson	1980–1981
Dr G.R. Chaudhry	1981–1982
S.D. Gera	1982–1983
Dr K.L. Gandhi	1983–1987
Dr N.N. Kher	1987–1992
I.B. Kapoor	1992–1994
Brig. K.S. Saghu	1994–1997
Vandana Puri	1998–2011
Sonia A. Verma	2011 to present

Salwan Social Welfare Centre

Recognizing the strong connection between education and society, the Trust opened the Salwan Welfare Centre in 1970 at J.J. Colony, Inderpuri, New Delhi.

Raj Salwan laying the foundation stone of the Salwan Social Welfare Centre in 1970.

This centre, which provides medical care and also vocational training, is now ushering in the new concept of a tertiary medical centre for the J.J. Colony. It is the students who will manage this centre, with the motto of 'Service Before Self.'

Gyan Devi Salwan College, Delhi University

The Trust took a bold step of establishing Gyan Devi Salwan College in the campus at Rajendra Nagar. The late Gyan Devi Salwan, wife of Girdhari Lal, was as passionate as her husband about the cause of education, and therefore bequeathed her assets to the Trust. 'All my cash, jewellery and other movable property whether in my bank account, locker or anywhere else shall be given to the Salwan Education Trust for building and running a college of the Trust.'

The college was affiliated to the Delhi University and was started in 1970. A block was made for the college, which ran in the evening, using the facilities of the Salwan Boys Senior Secondary School. Later, in 1983, the lieutenant governor of Delhi, Jagmohan, allotted 6.5 acres of land to the Trust at Inderpuri, near the Indian Council of Agricultural Research (Pusa Institute). Until the end of April 1983, the college was housed in a temporary building with Professor N.K. Jain as its first principal. The college may not have churned out great scholars but its sports team was one of the finest, especially in athletics. The credit went to the sports faculty and the students, who focused their power and resources on achievements in sports. Some of the finest national players were from Salwan College. Though it stood for a few years, it did create hope for many who were otherwise deprived of good higher education.

Considering the average student profile, Professor Jain met

the vice chancellor and told him, '"You give me 160 students from this area and only five students to Hindu College and you say that Hindu College is a good college! Reverse it and then see which college is better." The then vice chancellor, Prof R.C. Mehrotra, changed the rules and fixed a quota of 5 per cent of students from backward areas in all colleges. From the very first year, our commerce results proved to be excellent and in some respects we did better than Sri Ram College of Commerce. Our turnaround was better as we were admitting students with an average profile and churning out first class students.'

Another characteristic of the Salwan College, recalls Professor Jain, was that 'there was absolutely no interference in the working of the college, either in the admission process or in the fee concession structure. A noteworthy incident marked the beginning stages of the college when differences erupted between the university officials and the Salwan Education Trust regarding the first staff appointment. This led to bitter strife, with the university staff staging a walkout in some cases of appointment/recruitments. Shri Shiv Dutt's intentions of appointing on the basis of "merit" did not go down well with some university officials. They felt that he, like his father, was arrogant.'

A college in the school campus turned out to be a problematic proposition. It was difficult to control the male students, who indulged in the usual pranks of young collegiates. There was political interference. The matter went to the high court and then the Supreme Court. The Trust was allowed to construct a college building, but the interference continued. The Trust did not appreciate the dispute and political interference. It deliberated over the issue. The final decision was not to construct the college and instead it was shifted to Chanakyapuri in 1989 and named the Delhi College of Arts and Commerce. It is managed by the Delhi administration.

Gyan Devi Salwan Public School, Rajendra Nagar

Soon after the closure of the college and its shift from the Rajendra Nagar campus, the Board of Trustees decided to add another institution to the public school conglomerate under the name Gyan Devi Salwan Public School. This was in 1990.

This institute marked major additions and advancements not only on the infrastructure but also on the facilities' front in

Gyan Devi Salwan Public School, Rajendra Nagar.

a significant way. It is now that the wheel really came full circle with all forms of education in full bloom at the Integrated Education campus.

The school has evolved a unique methodology of imparting education via state-of-the-art technology and expertise. The school was given the British Council International School Award from 2007 to 2014. This school won the first position in the Global School Partnerships (since 2005) honours for the longest running partnership programme and second position in the best use of technology in developing sustaining partnerships by the British Council of India.

It bagged the 'Best National Green School Award in 2011-12' and ranked first at the national level for adopting the most innovative and effective practices to manage natural resources available within the premises. In a very short span of time, the school has created a unique place for itself. An emphasis on quality education and great teamwork makes this institution distinct from others.

His Holiness Gopal Krishna Goswami Maharaj of ISKCON Temple with Sushil Dutt during a visit to the school in 2011.

Today as one walks into the lush green campus of the school, hundreds of children can be seen busy with curricular and extracurricular activities. The school tries to inculcate respect for all vocations and professions in the students. The school is committed to nurturing vibrant human beings, who can think and act independently while contributing meaningfully to society. The students are groomed to be strong in mind, body and spirit—confident individuals who can give the right kind of leadership to India, an economic superpower in the making.

The following principals have contributed to the growth of the school—

Principals	Year
R. Suri	1990–1990
S. Dhingra	1990–1991
Asha Chiber	1991–1992
Romila Suri	1992–1995
Neera Chopra	1995–1997
Dr T. Sudha	1998–1999
Col Sham Dudeja	1999–2001
Mangla Sahni	2001–2004
Nirupma Kapoor	2004–2005
Rima C. Ailawadi	2005–2008
Vijay Laxmi Singh	2008 to present

Salwan Public School (Afternoon), Rajendra Nagar

As part of the Integrated Campus initiative, another public school was added to the list with the opening of the Salwan Public School (Afternoon) in 1991. The idea had its roots in

Shiv Dutt's trip to Kolkata in the late 1980s, when he visited the South Point School, which operated on a three-shift basis with a strength that was the largest in the world. When he returned, the idea was implanted and the experiment started in 1991.

As a pioneer, Salwan Public School (Afternoon) has not only excelled in academics but has also made a mark in various other fields. It has received the Green School Award from the Centre of Science and Environment in various categories every year since 2008. The beautification of the metro pillars at Pusa Road is the first and only project of its kind where Salwanians took the lead and transformed the cityscape into a beautiful potential tourist walk. The project, conceived by the students

Salwan Public School (Afternoon), Rajendra Nagar.

and approved by E. Sreedharan, former managing director of Delhi Metro, is appreciated by everyone.

The British Council division of Edinburgh recognized the efforts of the school and felicitated it with the International School Award for the period 2011-2014. Duke University, under its Duke Talent Identification Programme (TIP), has given scholarships to the students for attending training programmes at the best B-schools in India. There is an active ongoing exchange programme with Germany under which many students have availed scholarships for month-long study programmes.

Face-to-Faith Foundation, chaired by Tony Blair (former prime minister of the United Kingdom) conducts active video

Beautification of the Metro pillars at Rajendra Nagar by students of the Salwan Public School (Afternoon).

conferences with the school students as part of its campaign to achieve eradication of malaria from the world. They also exchange the best educational and cultural practices.

The girls volleyball team is the pride of the school as it has constantly won all the major tournaments at the national level. The school can proudly boast not only of enviable achievements in sports but in art too. Shivali Mittal won an award for her painting on 'Conservation of Energy' from the chief minister of Delhi and the president of India.

Shashi Bhanotia (TGT, Sanskrit) has been judged the 'best Sanskrit teacher' on four occasions by the Sanskrit Academy. She has also been awarded the 'Lifetime Achievement Award' for best performance in teaching of Sanskrit by the Delhi government.

Several individuals have spearheaded the school activities and allowed it to attain its present glory:

Principals	*Year*
Vandana Puri	1991–1998
Col. D.R. Mendiratta	1998–2003
K.L. Chopra	2003–2004
Dr S.P. Singh	2004–2005
Vijay Laxmi Singh	2005–2008
Rima C. Ailawadi	2008–2011
Mukul Jha	2012 to present

Having gone through the journey of the Salwan institutes at the Integrated Campus it becomes obvious that all the schools were initially based upon a unique rationale and over a period of time each school developed its own raison d'etre. The Rajendra Nagar campus can appropriately be looked upon as an excellent example of a 'Unison in separateness,' which made it a highly successful model with six schools spread over an area of 42,500 square metres housing 7,000 students. With this, the 'first phase of growth' was complete, and the second phase of expansion started.

Lighting the Satellites

Now the time had come to take the mission forward and to move from the core cluster to the satellites. The Trust decided to use the learning curve and apply it to other geographical locations for the benefit of society, thus carrying forward the mission and credo of Girdhari Lal. The vision became a reality with the first satellite unit coming up in Naraina in 1993.

Salwan Junior Public School, Naraina

When the land was first allotted, there was resistance from the neighbourhood. Little did they realize that this school would be a great boon and comfort zone for them. Though the neighbours filed a suit seeking injunction against the school building coming up, the same was dismissed by the court as the judge felt that there was nothing greater than education for this country, where millions remain uneducated even today.

The school was finally completed in 1993 and inaugurated by Raj Salwan. This was the first school of the Salwan Trust to get professional advice on design. The open spaces and big rooms gave a new dimension to school buildings.

Salwan Junior Public School, Naraina, offers education up to class V, after which the students are absorbed into the main branch at Rajendra Nagar for higher studies. The school spots talent in the juniors and prepares them for national- and state-

Salwan Junior Public School, Naraina.

level competitions in various activities such as judo, skating, martial arts, taekwondo, music and dance. The school is also known for its ballets and music concerts. It is also recognized for its contribution to community service and environmental projects.

The following principals have led the school:

Principals	*Year*
P. Verma	1993–1994
Neera Chopra	1994–1995
S. L. Gadi	1996–1999
S.R. Phillips	1999–2000
Poonam Chopra	2000–2002
Nisha Oberoi	2002 to present

Salwan Public School, Mayur Vihar

While the Salwan Education Trust was on the mission of enhancing the capacity to educate, it was also true that education was becoming more and more competitive,

Salwan Public School, Mayur Vihar.

demanding extra working hours for the students. Parents too realized that 'good enough' marks and grades were not enough and even fractions of a percentage could make or mar future prospects. While the Delhi campus at Rajendra Nagar attracted students from all over the National Capital Region, the management was aware that commuting time meant reduced time for self study. The Salwan School at Rajendra Nagar catered to students from trans-Yamuna and south Delhi areas, including Maharani Bagh. Realizing the dire need for another school, the Salwan Education Trust applied to the Delhi Development Authority (DDA) for allotment of space in a farflung area in east Delhi. The request was considered with 13,823 square metres of land being allocated. Consequently the first institute in east Delhi was started in 1996 as Salwan Public School, Mayur Vihar. It began on a humble note with just thirty-six students and two teachers. The school building's foundation stone was laid by Justice Davinder Gupta, who was a judge in the Delhi High Court. It is now a full-fledged school with well-equipped infrastructure, combined with innovative teaching methodology.

The school initiated path-breaking steps through an integrated approach. As part of these measures, the school has created a close-knit partnership with the British Council division for children and teachers to give a global dimension to the school curriculum. The school received the International School Award from the British Council for the years 2007-10 and 2011-14.

The school has been conducting Young Learners English Tests at different levels where every student is rewarded for his or her efforts by the Cambridge University. The teachers are trained and re-trained to develop competency in the education planning processes. The school offers an opportunity for the English teachers to undergo training for the Certificate in English Language Teaching (CELTA) Course conducted by the British Council. This programme enables the teachers to learn the new techniques of teaching English at elementary and international level and is entirely funded by the school. Partnership with the Reggio Emilia (Italy) has changed the outlook of Early Childhood educators towards new teaching-learning practices.

Kiran Mehta received the state award given by the Government of India for the year 2011 from Sheila Dikshit, chief minister of Delhi. Kiran Mehta has led the school since 1996.

Salwan Public School, Gurgaon

While the infrastructure was being consolidated in east Delhi, the management was eyeing yet another important part of the

Salwan Public School, Gurgaon.

NCR that was growing into a budding metropolis. Gurgaon had already started making waves with its ultramodern infrastructure. The Trust knew that quality education would be of utmost importance for the discerning parents of this Millennium City. The trigger for the Gurgaon School project was Dr S.Y. Qureshi, former director general of Doordarshan and later the chief election commissioner of India, who happened to attend a programme of the Salwan Public School (Afternoon), Rajendra Nagar. At that time, he was joint secretary, sports and youth affairs in the ministry of human resource development. He said that it was one of the best programmes he had witnessed. As if reading the thoughts of the management, he told Sushil Dutt Salwan that the Trust should not confine its educational activities to Delhi alone and suggested that they explore Gurgaon in Haryana where many corporates and multinational businesses were already moving. Sushil Dutt recalls, 'When I met him, he gave me very useful suggestions and words of wisdom. We are in Gurgaon today thanks to Dr Qureshi's advice. I acted on his suggestion and ventured into a new state for a new school. It took two years but God heard our prayers. We were allotted five acres of land by the Haryana Urban Development Authority (HUDA) in Sector 15, Phase II, Gurgaon.'

The construction of the school building started in 1995 and yet another beautiful edifice was completed the following year. Presently, there are 2500 students in this school and it is reported to be one of the best schools in the city.

The school is ISO 9001:2008 certified. True excellence is a

Dr Indu Khetarpal, principal of Salwan School, being honoured with the 'National Award for Teachers' in 2005 by President A.P.J. Abdul Kalam.

result of the combined efforts of the teachers and the students. The school seeks to continually improve the knowledge, social, cultural and academic skills of its students, while creating a conducive atmosphere for the budding leaders of tomorrow. An integrated approach in the teaching of all subjects is followed at the primary level. The school received the 'State Level Computer Literacy Excellence Award' for the year 2005 from the department of Information Technology, ministry of communication and information technology (MCIT), Government of India.

The school was awarded the 'National Values Award 2010' for the National Bal Bhawan Activities on 14 November by the Government of India.

The school also runs many IGNOU (Indira Gandhi National Open University) courses alongside the international curriculum.

Over the years the school has been led by the following principals:

Principals	*Year*
Dr Sunil Sondhi	1996–1997
Dr Indu Khetarpal	1997 to present

Salwan Montessori School, Gurgaon

The Salwan Education Trust believes that early childhood is a unique and important stage in a child's life. The Salwan Montessori School was set up with the goal of helping little children grow into confident, secure and empowered children. The school aims at excellence in pre-primary education by imparting holistic, activity-based education in a meaningful

Salwan Montessori School, Gurgaon.

learning environment. Efforts are on to make Salwan Montessori School an exclusive research centre in the field of Early Childhood Care and Education (ECCE). The school covers an area of 1000 square metres and has a strength of 250 students.

The curriculum of the school is development-oriented and child-centred. The school helps students realize their potential by providing an effective, calm and happy learning environment to enhance the six areas of learning. It aims to develop students who seek knowledge and understanding of their surroundings. A range of teacher-made material for all the concepts and computer-aided education makes learning enjoyable and exciting for the children. The methodology of teaching is integrated with other disciplines and children learn through direct hands-on experience with people, objects, events and ideas, thus providing an enriching experience for the children.

The school has made a special contribution by bringing out the first journal on ECCE, *Navtika*. This is a pioneering effort towards building a sound foundation for a progressive nation.

It was launched on 20 January 2007 by the joint secretary, ministry of women and child development, Government of India. This is the only Indian journal dealing with care and education in the age group of 0-8 years. It is published quarterly and features articles designed to impart new information and sharing of ideas among practitioners in the field of early childhood. The editorial board of the journal has eminent persons on its roll.

The school has won the 'All India Competition on Innovative Practices and Experiments in Schools and Teacher Education Institutions' organized by the National Council of Education Research and Training' in 2010. The topic was, 'Effect of story-centred approach for overall development during early childhood.'

The school has also participated in a national seminar on 'early literacy' organized by NCERT on 24 January 2012. Only twelve entries were selected for presentation from all over the country. The paper on 'Early Literacy Skills—Issues and Concerns', submitted by the school was selected for presentation.

The following principals have led the school:

Principals	Year
Roopali Pandey	1999–2000
Amita Tandon	2000–2009
Moushumi Bose	2009 to present

Salwan Public School, Tronica City

Salwan Public School, Tronica City, was established in July 2005. The school is situated on a ten-acre plot. The school stands for excellence in education with great emphasis on its students being good human beings. The school has adopted the play-

Salwan Public School, Tronica City.

way and activity-oriented approach to teaching and learning. 'Every child matters as every child is special' is the guiding belief, and teachers are guides and facilitators and learn as much from students as vice-versa. Besides academics, the students are also trained in gymnastics, roller skating, taekwondo, cricket, football, volleyball, yoga, art and craft, music, dance, theatre and athletics on a daily basis. Summer camps and adventure camps are organized during the vacations wherein the students are coached in all co- and co-scholastic activities. Disaster management drills and educational trips are a regular feature. Leadership training is undertaken for both primary as well as secondary classes. Various inter-class and inter-house competitions are organized to foster critical and creative thinking skills. Respect for Mother Nature is inculcated right from early childhood.

The students love the free expression class in art and dance.

Class-wise weekly picnic lunches on sprawling school lawns and yoga for each child constitutes the 'happiness class', which forms an essential factor for evaluation. The curriculum caters to the multiple intelligence theory and is interdisciplinary and based on the project-method as well as the problem-solving approach.

The challenges the Trust faced here were different. With no inhabitation in the neighbouring area and first generation learners coming to regular school, the Trust took this challenge and venture very sportingly. It did not compromise on anything. Teachers were transported from Delhi to ensure quality education. The school grew from a strength of thirty-five students in the first year to more than 700 students in a short span of seven years. It has staged four mega cultural programmes and one Hot Weather Cricket Tournament. The CBSE Cluster Girls Athletic meet was also hosted by the school in 2012.

Venturing into this tough terrain, the following individuals have led the school:

Principals	Year
S.R. Phillips	2005–2006
Shubha Gill	2006–2010
Premila Sharma	2010–2012
Rajni Jauhari	2012 to present

Good and effective management is the core strength of all great institutions. The secretaries of the Trust play a vital role in paving a dynamic path for competent administration. The Trust has been very fortunate on this account and has had the following secretaries, whose contribution is immeasureable:

Fakir Chand Marwah	1948–1965
J.R. Mullick	1965–1980
B.R. Vyas	1981–1986
L.D. Gupta	1987–2006
Paramjit Khanna	2006 to present

The Salwan Education Trust Today

The Salwan Education Trust has always had eminent people on its Board of Governors. The tradition of constituting the governing body of the Trust with able and distinguished members is practised even today. At present, the Salwan Education Trust is managed by members from different walks of life; they include educationists, members of the judiciary, bankers and corporate heads and army officers. Their names are:

- S.D. Salwan, philanthropist and social worker
- Justice P.N. Khanna, former judge, Delhi High Court
- Justice Jaspal Singh, former judge, Delhi High Court
- Justice Manmohan Sarin, Lokayukt, NCT of Delhi and former chief justice, J&K High Court
- B.L. Khurana, former chairman, New Bank of India
- A.P. Paracer, additional director general (retd.), CPWD
- Harpal Singh, chairman emeritus, Fortis Health Care Ltd.
- Maj Gen J.K. Kapoor (retd.), consultant, automobile industry
- Lt Gen Arvind Mahajan, former DG, EME
- Inder Dutt Salwan, architect
- Anusuya Salwan, LLM, advocate
- Sushil Dutt Salwan, advocate
- Dr Roopa Salwan, MD (Med), DM (Cardiology)
- Paramjit Khanna, chartered accountant
- Janak Juneja, IAS (retd.)
- Dr Indu Khetarpal, educationist

MEMBERS OF THE SALWAN EDUCATION TRUST

*From left to right (Sitting): Lt Gen (Retd.) Arvind Mahajan, A.P. Paracer,
Justice Jaspal Singh, S.D. Salwan, Harpal Singh, Maj Gen (Retd.) J.K. Kapoor,
Justice Manmohan Sarin, B.L. Khurana. From left to right (Standing):
Maj (Retd.) S.K. Kohli, (Director, HRD, SET), Anusuya Salwan, Dr Indu Khetarpal,
Sushil Dutt Salwan, Paramjit Khanna, Dr Roopa Salwan.*

Inder Dutt Salwan   *Janak Juneja*   *Justice P.N. Khanna*

*At the Golden Jubilee Celebration of the Trust. (Left to Right): Shiv Dutt Salwan,
S.D. Varma, B.L. Khurana, Justice P.N. Khanna, T.R. Tuli, Lt Gen (Retd.) H.S. Seth,
R.C. Pandey, Brig (Retd.) M.L. Khetarpal and Brig (Retd.) K.N. Singh.*

*Madhavrao Scindia with Shiv Dutt Salwan at the Golden Jubilee Celebrations of
Salwan Education Trust.*

Many trustees, during their lifetime, have made significant contributions to the growth and development of the Trust and its activities. Nobody can replace them and they shall always be remembered and thanked by the staff and students of all the schools. Besides those who served during Girdhari Lal's time, other prominent trustees have been Sardar Hardyal Singh, M.R. Kohli, chairman New Bank of India, Justice N.C. Kochhar, Ramesh Dutt Salwan, Sardar Harnam Singh Suri, Chief Justice Hardyal Hardy, Hardayal Devgun, Justice H.L. Anand, Dr A.S. Paintal, former director, Patel Chest Institute, T.R. Tuli, former chairman, Punjab National Bank, Justice Prithvi Raj, Justice S.S. Daulat, S.D. Varma, former chairman, Allahabad Bank, Justice G.C. Jain, D.R. Gandotra, chairman, New Bank of India.

On the 110th birth anniversary of Girdhari Lal Salwan, the ministry of communication and information department of posts, Delhi, brought out a special cover as a tribute to him.

Salwan Education Trust's Vision

The Salwan Education Trust made certain seminal contributions in the service of school education. The core values of the Trust impel all to dedicate themselves to building a world in which everyone's basic human needs are met. Sushil Dutt Salwan says, 'While the Right of Children to Free and Compulsory Education Act received the assent of the president of India fairly recently on 26 August 2009, the manifestations of the same were echoed in strong measure through the vision of Girdhari Lal Salwan way back in 1949 and has been carried forth as a cherished legacy of the founder through the philosophy, policies, practice and code of conduct established by the Trust.'

Also, the development of the education hub at Rajendra Nagar created a platform for common infrastructure and a pool of valued resources. The government-aided schools were housed in the same campus with equal infrastructure and facilities, common teacher training resources, shared playgrounds and sports facilities as if anticipating the stipulation of the Act almost sixty two years ago.

The policies of the Salwan institutions are exemplary edicts of the morals that form the principles of the Trust. The policies of the founder are being scrupulously adhered to. As per precedant set by Pandit Girdhari Lal, no trustee takes any monetory benefit from the Trust or school funds. Every penny saved is ploughed back into the system for the benefit of the students. This honesty is responsible for the growth and expansion of the institutions. The directors of the schools, being professionals, manage all issues in a highly effective and transparent manner, with great competence, keeping the interest of the children and teachers paramount. Sushil Dutt quotes Robert F. Kennedy: 'Few will have the greatness to change history itself but each one of us can work to change a small portion of events, and in the total of all those acts will be written the history of this generation.'

The core institutional values which the Trust strives to develop and sustain in all its programmes and activities are:

- Commitment
- Creativity
- Motivation
- Efficiency
- Effectiveness
- Excellence
- Individual freedom
- Responsiveness to societal needs
- Diversity with synergy

What is the difference between school and life outside of it? In school, you are taught a lesson and then you give a test. In life, you are given a test that teaches you a lesson. Our educational institutions will not be judged only by standards which are linked with infrastructure or the quality of teachers or exam outcomes, but also by whether the children get the opportunities to realize their potential.

The barriers and roadblocks that we face are usually in our minds and these can be demolished by having the determination to find a solution, even one that runs contrary to conventional wisdom. The man who knows how to do this will always have a job and the man who knows why will always be the leader.

Sushil Dutt Salwan says, 'I am a strong believer in creative philanthropy. It is an approach that allows sustained institutionalized philanthropy for long-term, high-impact socioeconomic transformation. The avenues of change can be many but I believe that education has the power to be the single largest tool for this purpose.'

The Salwan Girls and Salwan Boys schools are social initiatives conceived of by Girdhari Lal Salwan to provide 'Education for All'. This model is perhaps the only correct solution and a most appropriate answer to the implementation difficulties of the concept of Right to Education for all. The Salwan Girls and Boys Schools are not schools for the underprivileged, but state-of-the-art institutions that address social imbalances and nurture leaders for tomorrow. It is a model that can be scaled up and replicated globally to create philanthropic institutions of lasting relevance and impact. The Trust should continue to nourish them further through the influx of knowledge sources, funds and greater commitment in all spheres.

The members of the Trust have pledged to actively pursue the vision plan to make their institutions a global destination for research, training and teaching in education. The Trust will diversify its academic initiatives while focusing on:

Research: An institution of excellence is driven by knowledge rather than demand. Research is at the heart of all intellectual activities. The Salwan Schools will be research oriented, with great focus on the science stream.

State-of-the-Art Curriculum: The endeavour is for the best international standard curriculum within an engaging and inquiry-based environment.

Pedagogy: The schools will utilize the newest versions of instructional strategies and the latest technology in education.

Image: They will strive to be among the top global schools of excellence.

Acquisition: Acquire schools in other parts of the country.

Hallmark of excellence: The schools are being restructured. While one of them will have an international curriculum, others will include a centre for excellence in science and research, a residential school as well as a school-cum-sports academy modelled to earn the distinction of being the national leader in sports.

Sushil Dutt believes that he represents a generation that wants to rewrite the script. He accepts that those who expect to reap the blessings of glory must undergo the fatigue of creating it first. He has learnt that success does not consist of never making mistakes but in never making the same one twice. Girdhari Lal lived life on his own terms, and bequeathed to the world a legacy. 'As his heirs, we bear the moral responsibility to keep alive these temples of wisdom and build further as part of the mission "Education for All!"'

Index